FIVE MEN *of* BURGH

CONTENTS

OPPOSITE

Inscription on the war memorial at St Botolph's Church, Burgh, Suffolk.

The 11th November 2018 will mark the centenary of the end of the Great War of 1914 to 1918. It was described at the time as "*the war to end all wars*", with over eighteen million deaths in total[1]. However, an even more widespread and destructive war was to break out only 21 years later, with over sixty million deaths[2]. This became known as the Second World War with The Great War becoming known as the First World War or World War I.

Although the total number of casualties of all nations was far higher in the Second World War, Britain itself suffered a far higher number of deaths in the Great War. The number of British dead in the Second World War, according to a recent Commonwealth War Graves Commission report, was 383,718, just under one per cent of the population[3].

The number of the nation's dead in the Great War was demonstrated by the display of ceramic poppies at the Tower of London in 2014, *Blood Swept Lands and Seas of Red.* Each poppy represented one of the British dead. A total of 888,246 poppies[4] was used, based on Commonwealth War Graves Commission figures from 2010-2011, though this included some casualties from Britain's overseas territories.

The Commission's more recent report, for 2013-14, adjusts this figure to a total of 887,711 dead for the United Kingdom alone, nearly two per cent of the national population in 1911[5].

The vast majority of the British casualties in the Great War were suffered in France and Flanders, on the Western Front. By late 1914, the fighting in this theatre had evolved into two parallel lines of trenches and fortifications, stretching from the Belgian coast down to the Swiss border. The British and Allied forces on one side faced the German forces on the other, across no-man's land. From late 1914 through to early 1918, repeated offensives by either side failed to make a major breakthrough against the entrenched forces facing them, incurring huge numbers of casualties for both attackers and defenders. Many of these casualties were caused by machine gun fire or artillery bombardment, but the fighting also saw the widespread use of poison gas and the emergence of new weapons, such as tanks and aircraft.

The scale and manner of British losses on the Western Front remains shocking and difficult to comprehend to the present day.

The war memorial situated beside the parish church of St Botolph at Burgh in Suffolk (*fig. 1*) is inscribed with the names of five men who died in the Great War, with three further names added after the Second World War. The five men who died in the Great War represent about two and a half per cent of the 1911 population of Burgh, which was 212 persons, according to the census that year[6]. Five out of two hundred or so is a similar rate of losses to the two per cent mortality rate suffered by Britain as a whole, so the experience of Burgh would seem typical of small villages up and down the land.

Each year of the Great War saw the death of another of the five men listed on the village war memorial and their individual stories reflect the progress of the war for the British, from the initial reliance in 1914 upon the soldiers of the pre-war army, followed by a huge rush of volunteers, many of whom were to lose their lives on the Western Front. Whilst terrible losses were being suffered on the Somme and around Ypres, offensives were also launched at Gallipoli and in Mesopotamia (modern day Iraq) between 1915 and 1917. Early 1918 then saw the Germans launch major offensives, before the Allies drove them decisively back, leading to the signing of the Armistice, ending the fighting, on 11 November 1918.

The parish church also contains a Roll of Honour, which includes the names of the men of the village who served in the war and survived: see Chapter 5.

Burgh's war memorial also lists the names of three servicemen who died in the Second World War. Researching Second World

BELOW

*The war memorial
at St Botolph's Church,
Burgh, Suffolk.*

War servicemen tends to be more difficult than those of the Great War, as more recent service and census records are not yet generally available to the public. Nonetheless, some details have been found for these three men and these follow in Chapter 7.

The Commonwealth War Graves Commission also records three further casualties of the two wars, associated with Burgh, as described in Chapters 3 and 8.

CHAPTER 1

FIVE MEN OF BURGH
The Great War Fallen

PRIVATE HERBERT GEORGE HUGHES

No. 1491 The Black Watch (Royal Highlanders)
Died 12th December 1914, aged 27

Herbert Hughes was born at Kirton in Suffolk in 1887, the son of Charles and Lizzie Hughes. Charles was an agricultural labourer, born at Levington, while Lizzie (formerly Lizzie Marsh) was from Bottisham in Cambridgeshire. They had ten children, of whom eight appear to have survived infancy. Herbert was their second son.

By 1891, the family, with the first three children, was living at Falkenham (*fig. 2*).

The 1901 census indicates that they lived at Trimley for several years, where three more of the children were born, before moving to Waldringfield in about 1900, with Charles now a labourer at a cement factory[7]. However, Herbert had by then already left home and, aged only 13, shows up as a carpenter's labourer boarding in lodgings at New Street, Woodbridge, Suffolk. (*fig. 3*).

The records indicate that Herbert enlisted with the Black Watch Regiment at Lochgelly, Fifeshire, Scotland[8], in 1908.

By 1911, he was serving with the regiment in India (*fig. 4*), whilst his parents and family were living at Judgments Farm, Wattisham, Suffolk[9].

Following heavy losses at the beginning of the war, in October 1914 the British Expeditionary Force in France and Belgium was reinforced by brigades of troops brought over from India, known as "Indian Expeditionary Force A". These included the 7th (Meerut) Division, one battalion of which was the 2nd Battalion, Black Watch (Royal Highlanders), in which Herbert Hughes was serving as a private[10].

The battalion left its station at Bareilly in India on 3rd September 1914, bound for Karachi, from where it embarked on the 16th September, proceeding via the Red Sea and Suez Canal to Marseilles, where the battalion disembarked on October 12th. On the 20th October 1914, the battalion moved north by train to Orleans to join the rest of the Meerut Division[11,12]. Fierce fighting was ongoing in the sector around Ypres in Belgium, stretching southwards towards La Bassée and Bethune in northern France.

The regimental history for the Black Watch records:

> "In these circumstances there was no time for the Indian Corps to assemble as a whole or to be given any period of preparation for the conditions in which it was to fight. It had to be employed to meet an emergency.....Thus the Battalion, leaving Orleans on October

26th, detrained north of Lillers, and marched at once up to the front line....the Meerut Division was used to relieve a part of the II Corps, which had borne the brunt of the fighting during the retreat from Mons, had been heavily engaged on the Aisne and by La Bassée, and was sorely in need of a rest.

On the night of the 29th the Bareilly Brigade took over the extreme right of the British line...

The front line held by the Battalion consisted of a single trench, some 800 to 1000 yards east of the village of Le Plantin...

The first few days in the line passed without incident, so far as the Battalion was concerned; but a little further north, on the left of the Bareilly Brigade, the 2/8th Gurkhas were attacked almost immediately after the occupation of the trenches, and suffered severely, losing nine of their British officers. Owing to this, The Black Watch was, on November 2nd, called on to send its Headquarters and the two reserve companies (Nos. 1 and 2, which had been relieved in the front line by 3 and 4 on November 1st), to take over a part of the line further north; and for the remainder of its first tour in trenches, which lasted till the third week in November, the Battalion was split up, Headquarters and Nos. 1 and 2 Companies being in the left section of the Bareilly Brigade, while Nos. 3 and 4 remained in the original trenches north of Givenchy, on the right of the line...

The chief incident in the left section was a night raid made on the German trenches by some twenty men of No. 2 Company under Captain Forrester, with the object of destroying a machine gun which was causing annoyance from a sap pushed up close to our line. The raid took place on November 9th. Captain Forrester was wounded through the lungs as the raid started, but continued to lead his men, who reached the German trenches and killed ten of the enemy in hand-to-hand fighting; the machine gun had, however, been removed. The party returned with Captain Forrester, Sergeant Wallace and one private wounded"[13].

No further action is recorded for the battalion until the 17th November 1914.

Herbert Hughes is recorded as having died of wounds at Number 6 Casualty Clearing Hospital, Bethune, France, on 12th November 1914 (*fig. 5*). Bethune is just south of the Belgian border. He is buried at Bethune Cemetery[14] (*figs. 6 and 7*). Perhaps he was the wounded private referred to in the above extract from the regimental history, but other men from his battalion are buried nearby who also died between 9th and 17th November, so it is impossible to be sure for the time being (at the time of writing, the battalion war diary, which could perhaps provide more details, is unavailable at the National Archives, having been removed for digitisation).

So the question arises as to what connection Herbert Hughes has with Burgh. In this regard, his parents Charles and Lizzie appear to have moved to Seven Gardens, Burgh, by 1919, from where Charles requested the inscription "GONE BUT NOT FORGOTTEN" for Herbert's headstone at Bethune (*fig. 8*).

Charles died locally in 1926[15] and Lizzie in Ipswich in 1935[16].

The war memorial at Falkland in Fife, Scotland[17] lists a "Private Bert Hughes", which may also be a reference to Herbert Hughes.

Herbert's brother, Frederick John Hughes, born in 1900 at Waldringfield, Suffolk, would later become a Gunner in the Royal Artillery, but was sadly killed at sea in 1941, being listed on the Plymouth Naval Memorial[18].

PRIVATE ALBERT VICTOR LAST

*No. 15058, 9th Battalion, Suffolk Regiment
Died 30th December 1915, aged 18*

Albert Last was born in Cardiff, his birth being registered in early 1897. His father was William Last, who was born in Burgh, but at the time of Albert's birth was serving in the Welsh (traditionally 'Welch') Regiment. Albert's mother was Annie Friend, born at Clopton, a village next to Burgh.

In 1871, both William and Annie were living in Burgh, so it seems likely that they knew each other from childhood, even though their marriage in 1885 was in Cardiff.

Albert was the sixth of nine children, five girls and four boys, all born in Cardiff between 1886 and 1906. All the children were recorded as living in the 1911 census.

In both 1891 and 1901, the census shows the family living in barracks at Cardiff. In 1891, William was a corporal. By 1901, he had become a sergeant (*fig. 9*) and Albert was now shown as present in the household for the first time, aged five. Albert and his older brothers and sisters, particularly, would have been very familiar with military life.

At some point after the birth of their youngest son, Ernest, in 1905/6, William and Annie moved back to Burgh. William's army service had ended and he became sub-postmaster at the village post office, this being his occupation shown in the 1911 census (*figs. 10 and 11*). Albert was still living at home at this point, as a school pupil, but at some point after 1911 he appears to have become a railway clerk at nearby Little Bealings station (as stated in the newspaper report of his death, see further below).

The war now intervened.

The British Expeditionary Force (BEF) which landed in France at the outbreak of war totalled about 85,000 men[19].

As the strength of the BEF declined (casualty figures by the end of 1914 totalled over 90,000[20]), its numbers were first made up by the Territorial Force and troops from Britain's Imperial forces (such as the Indian brigades in which Herbert Hughes served). However, alongside this, a massive recruitment drive for volunteers was also undertaken, spearheaded by Field Marshal Kitchener (*fig. 12*). After a relatively slow start, there was a sudden surge in recruitment in late August and early September 1914. In all, 478,893 men joined the army between 4th

August and 12th September 1914, including 33,204 on 3 September alone – the highest daily total of the war and more in one day than the average yearly intake in the years immediately before 1914[21].

By the end of September 1914, over 750,000 men had enlisted in the New Army[22]. By the end of World War I, almost one in four of the total male population of the United Kingdom of Great Britain and Ireland would join up, over five million men. Of these, 2.67 million joined as volunteers[23].

Many of the volunteers were enlisted into "Service" Battalions, formed of about a thousand men, newly created for service in the War. One such new battalion was the 9th Battalion of the Suffolk Regiment, the "9th Suffolks", which was formed at Bury St Edmunds in September 1914[24].

From Albert Last's service number, we know that he enlisted as a volunteer with the 9th Battalion in mid-September 1914[25]. He appears to have joined the Signalling section (see further below), so perhaps it was his experience as a railway clerk which led him in this direction[26].

Upon their formation, the 9th Suffolks were stationed at Shoreham in Sussex, as part of the 71st Brigade within the 24th Division (*fig. 13*). The inadequate facilities at Shoreham to cope with the huge number of recruits meant the men remained in tents until late November 1914, when wooden huts were constructed. Nonetheless, the battalion were moved into billets in Brighton over the winter, before returning to Shoreham in March 1915.

The 9th Suffolks also included in their number Ned Goodchild of Grundisburgh. The letters and postcards home of Ned and his brother Arthur mention Albert Last and other local volunteers in 'Kitchener's Army'. Arthur Goodchild's 's postcard of 24th November 1914 refers to Albert Last receiving punishment of seven days in camp for a minor disciplinary offence. Ned Goodchild's letter home to his mother of 8 March 1915 includes "I saw Albert Last Sat[urday] night for the first time in Brighton, he tells me George Chaplin is killed at the front, so he has soon done his bit towards his country".

Ned Goodchild was to be killed on the Western Front just ten days before Albert Last[27].

Training continued in the Shoreham area until late June 1915, when the battalion moved to Blackdown Camp, near Farnborough, to complete training. At this point, the battalion had yet to be issued with their service rifles, but they finally received these in July and began training with these on the rifle ranges at Bisley[28].

Having completed training, the battalion crossed from Folkestone to Boulogne on the night of 30th August 1915. They were then conveyed by train to Montreuil, about seven miles south-east of Etaples. From Montreuil they marched a few miles north to Alette. This was to be their base for three weeks, billeted in farm buildings[29].

At the front, the Spring of 1915 had brought a German offensive at Ypres, commencing on 22nd April 1915, where the assault began with the first use of poison gas on the Western Front, by the Germans against the French. The French line had disintegrated under this attack but, with the help of Canadian forces, the Germans had been prevented from pressing home their advantage. The British had then launched minor offensives at Aubers and Festubert in May 1915, but these failed, with heavy casualties, and the British command came under pressure from the French to launch a major offensive, even though there were serious doubts in the British command as to their readiness. Nonetheless, it was decided that an attack would take place against the German line north of the Belgian town of Loos. Final detailed orders for this were issued on 19th September 1915[30]. The assault was to include the 9th Suffolks, as part of the 24th Division. After only three weeks in France, the 9th Suffolks were now ordered to march nearly 70 miles to the front line, whilst a four-day artillery bombardment of the German line began.

The regiment's Official History[31] states:

> "During the night of 21-22 September the battalion set out for Matringhem. Continuing their journey on the following night, they reached Ham-en-Artois at three in the morning, where one of the companies found that its billets consisted of a tumbledown barn and a pigstye. However, at seven o'clock the battalion moved over to Le Cornet Bourdois, where they secured billets in the brigade concentration area. The next night, the march was resumed.

Another dawn found them all tired out, with "only a mile to go". Without orders, the whole battalion fell out and sat down by the roadside. One of their officers, a gallant but fiery major, told them they were "a d------d rotten mob" and that he was ashamed of them. The major's forcible style being well known, his outburst was taken in good part, and after each man had been served with a mug of tea, the journey was continued without a murmur to Bethune*, where they were comfortably quartered in barracks. The march from the coast had been an exceptionally trying one. The battalion had been on the move in drenching rain for four nights in succession, covering a distance of nearly seventy miles, and now within a few hours of their arrival in Bethune they were ordered to move again. But great occasions demand great efforts, and, in the presence of Field-Marshal Sir John French, the division set out from the market square in the highest spirits for the front."

*[nb. The Town Cemetery of Bethune is where Herbert Hughes is buried.]

The plan for the attack at Loos, devised by General Haig, was for an infantry assault on the 25th September 1915, to be followed by reserve troops, including the 9th Suffolks, on the 26th September. Once the first German position had fallen, the reserves, aided by cavalry, were to pass through the gap and attack the German second line.

The infantry assault went ahead as planned on 25th September 1915. Partly to make up for a shortage of available artillery to support such a large attack as had been planned, gas was used by the British in this attack for the first time (*fig. 14*). However, unfavourable wind conditions gave mixed results, resulting in the gas being blown back to the British lines in some places.

The southern section of the attack made significant progress on the first day of the battle, capturing Loos and moving onwards towards nearby Lens, but supply problems and a need for reserves brought the advance to a halt at the end of the first day. Haig had asked the British Commander-in-Chief, Sir John French, to make the reserve troops (including the 9th Suffolks) available for use the same day, but after resistance from French (perhaps appreciating the long march some of them had just endured), they were only eventually released during the early afternoon and then delays whilst travelling meant they only arrived at night.

The 9th Suffolks' war diary[32] illustrates the confusion of battle:

"25/9/15, 8pm, The Battalion was moved up in double line of platoons A & B in front, C & D in rear. A steady advance was made in this formation until the third and second lines of English trenches. On reaching the first line English and first line German trenches the Battalion was halted owing to an order coming from in front to retire...

About midnight the advance was held up for reasons then unknown and between that hour and dawn the Battalion dug trenches in advance of German rear trench...

26/9/15, 5 am...at dawn the Battalion was ordered back to the German support trench and occupied this. During the early hours of the day these trenches were occupied also the communication trenches.

26/9/15...at 11.25am an order was received that 21st & 24th Divisions should attack at 11 A.M [ie., 25 minutes before the order was received!], 21st on right 24th on left. The 72nd Brigade was detailed to attack the front allotted to 24th Division, with 11th Essex and 9th Suffolks in support, Suffolks on right, Essex on left, 600 yards in rear of 72nd Brigade. The original of this order was subsequently lost.

As the message was so late Lieutenant Colonel Brettell at once sent down verbal messages for immediate advance and each section mounted the parapet and advanced under a heavy shrapnel fire towards the objective named in the order of the previous evening [Vendin-le-Vieil]. Owing to the lack of time it was impossible to rally companies and organise the line but the various commanders did all they could during the advance to consolidate their units. A & C Companies were on the left B & D [one of these two companies containing Albert Last - see further below] on the right, some of each company being in the line. Owing to parts of the line being very far behind owing to late warning a very rapid advance had to be made on the left and it was found to be impossible to continue wearing packs and these were taken off. The advance continued until the HULLUCH - LENS Road was reached*. [inserted in the diary here: "*The leading line advanced about 150 to 200 yards beyond this road"]. Here the advance was held up for reasons then unknown and shortly afterwards the right flank began to retire. The centre held in to the road for about three hours and the flanks advanced and retired twice finally retiring about 5 P.M. the centre following and retiring to the German support trench which was held during the night. The left flank reported that they had come under enfillade machine gun fire [inserted: "from HULLUCH"] and were forced to retire and here most of the casualties occurred. Both the Commanding Officer and Adjutant were wounded and the orders were not recovered up to date of writing. An act of gallantry by Capt Charles Packard was reported to the Brigadier the following day.

7.0 P.M. [The] remaining portion of Battalion under Capt Packard (3 officers and 100 men) was ordered to hold the enemy's second line against counter-attacks and hold on until relieved. At about 8.30 the trench was occupied and the usual measures of conversion and defence were carried out with all dispatch.

No attack was carried out during the night. Just before being relieved Capt Packard got in touch with another party of the Battalion under Lieutenant Church.

27/9/15, 2.0 A.M

The party under Capt Packard was relieved by a company of Coldstream Guards and returned towards Vermelles. Owing to the late hour the men were bivouacked for the rest of the night joining the remainder of the Battalion at the Brigade encampment at SAILLY LABOURSE

9.30 A.M.

The roll of the Battalion was called and the absentees duly recorded. As far as could be ascertained the following were casualties among officers:

Killed: Lieut. T.T.Stevens

Wounded: Lt. Col. R.V.Brettell, Maj L.C.Arbuthnot, Capt & Adj. F. Hedges, Capt H.F.Law, Lt. R.England, Lt. F.R.Cobbold Casualties - Men: 9 killed, Died of wounds 2, Wounded 81, Missing 45."

[see Fig. 15 for part of the above extract]

So ended the involvement of the 9th Suffolks at Loos.

This was a baptism of fire for the battalion, going straight into battle after a long march, with no previous front-line experience, though many other battalions taking part in the attack suffered significantly greater casualties. the battle also saw the battalion's first Victoria Cross of the War, awarded to Sergeant Arthur Frederick Saunders[33].

Further attacks were carried out at Loos over the next three weeks, but by mid-October 1915, the Battle of Loos was effectively over, with minimal gains having been achieved at great cost. More than 61,000 British casualties were sustained. Of these, 7,766 men died[34].

Harold Macmillan, future prime minister but then a junior officer in the Guards Division, composed mostly of war-experienced troops, which followed the Suffolks into the line, later remarked in his autobiography:

> *I can still remember vividly this march from Vermelles to Loos.*
> *I must confess that for many months and even years I would*
> *dream of it ... What was distressing for our men was that the*
> *whole ground that we covered in our march was filled, or seemed*
> *to be filled, with the remnants of troops who had attacked in*
> *the earlier days of the battle ... [There] were the men of the 21st*
> *and 24th. Some were dead, some wounded, some broken and*
> *having lost all discipline or order. I have often wondered since*
> *why the decision was made to put in these divisions, who had*
> *never seen a shot fired and come straight from England, ahead of*
> *the Guards Division. It seemed a fatal error.*[35]

Having been relieved, the 9th Suffolks were then rested behind the front at Proven. For them, the battle of Loos was over and Albert Last was one of the survivors.

However, there was little rest, as the battalion marched north to the Ypres salient on 5th October 1915.

The regimental history[36] describes the conditions:

> The remainder of the year was spent in the [Ypres] Salient, the battalion occupying the line at Forward Cottage trenches or at St Jean. The weather was atrocious and the period as a whole indescribably wretched and trying for everyone. When not actually in the line the battalion was at or near Poperinghe, furnishing everlasting working parties at night, which had to grope their way up to the front in rain, mud, and darkness, and under persistent shell-fire. All ranks were constantly exercised in the rapid manipulation of gas-marks in anticipation of gas attacks.
> ....On December 19, while the battalion was in trenches in front of St Jean, the enemy again became active. Gas was sent over early in the morning, followed by a very heavy bombardment lasting twenty-four hours....the casualties in the battalion amounted to over eighty....the 9th Battalion was the first unit of the new armies to experience and withstand a gas attack...

After being relieved on the 23rd December 1915 and resting through Christmas Day that year, the battalion went back into the trenches at St Jean, just east of Ypres on 27 December 1915.

It was in this spell of a few days at the front that Albert Last was killed, on 30 December 1915. The battalion war diary for 30th December just states:

"In trenches - Battalion relieved. Relief completed without casualties at 8.30 P.M. Casualties O.R.[other ranks] Killed 1, Wounded 2" (fig. 16)

Albert's death was reported in the Suffolk Chronicle and Mercury on 7th January 1916 (*fig. 17*), which set out the text of his commanding officer's, Captain Lionel Ensor's, letter to his parents (*fig. 18*)[37], giving details of his death:

"It is my painful duty to inform you that your son was killed in action on December 30. Your boy died at his post, and did not suffer, death being instantaneous. He was hit in the head by part of a shell, while in the trenches with my company. Your boy was one of the best of soldiers: he always carried out his duties cheerfully and well, however hard the conditions, and was ready at all times to help out a comrade, should an opportunity occur".

The newspaper also referred to Albert's employment as a railway clerk and that he was in the Signalling section within his battalion (which role is also mentioned in the Goodchild letters[38]).

A further local newspaper item (*fig. 19*) contains a photograph of Albert and reference to him as having served in 'D' Company of his battalion, though the Commonwealth War Graves Commission, shows him as having been in 'B' Company.

Albert Last was 18 when he died and he is buried at White House Cemetery, Ypres (*figs. 20 and 21*). His family chose the inscription "AT REST" for his headstone (*fig. 22*).

The Suffolk Chronicle and Mercury of 11 January 1918 contained a memorial to Albert from his family (*fig. 23*) including the verse:

"His cheerful smile, his loving face, No one on earth can fill his place."

Albert's older brother Stanley also fought in the Great War, serving like his father in the Welch Regiment[39]. It is assumed that he survived the War, if only by not being listed on the Burgh war memorial. Albert's father William appears to have died in 1928[40]. There is a death registered in the Woodbridge registration district for an Annie Last in 1923, which may refer to Albert's mother[41].

LANCE CORPORAL WILLIAM
GLADSTONE CHENERY

No. 9039, 9th Battalion, Suffolk Regiment
Died 16th September 1916, aged 23

William Chenery was born at Kirton in 1893, the son of William and Eliza Chenery. William senior was a bootmaker, born at Debenham in about 1864, whilst Eliza, formerly Eliza Tye[42], was born at Burgh in about 1860. William junior had one sister, Alice Maud, born in 1886[43].

In 1901, the family was at Seven Gardens Road, Burgh (*fig. 24*), though William's sister Alice had moved away by then[44].

In 1911, William senior and Eliza remained in Burgh[45], with a grandson 8 months old, Harry William, presumably Alice's son, but by now William junior was serving as a private at Aldershot with the 2nd Battalion of the Suffolk Regiment (*fig. 25*). His service number indicates that he joined the Regiment in 1910[46].

William's circumstances in the first months of the War are not clear. What we do know is that, in April 1915, he was at Felixstowe where, as a lance corporal, he took part in a football match between Felixstowe Garrison and the "Corinthians under arms" (*fig. 26*). The 3rd (Reserve) Battalion of the Suffolk Regiment were based at Felixstowe Garrison at this time[47], supplying drafts for front-line units, so perhaps William's original term of service with the 2nd Suffolks had ended, but he had rejoined the Regiment and been placed in the Felixstowe Garrison due to his previous military experience.

In any event, in October 1915, Ned Goodchild of Grundisburgh, serving in the 9th Suffolks, wrote home to his mother from the Ypres Salient on 16th October 1915: "...Bill Chenery is in our Coy. too, he came with the last draft from Felixstowe..."[48]. So, like Albert Last, William was now joining the 9th Suffolks.

Ned Goodchild's letter of 21 November 1915 to his brother George mentions William as having been slightly wounded: "Will Chenery from Burgh is in our lot now......he had his overcoat rent in several places by some shrapnel and a small wound in his arm but not enough to go to Bli[gh]ty."

Booth's Almanac for 1916[49], which gives a roll of honour for Burgh, has "frostbitten" against William Chenery's name. It is assumed that this would have been suffered by William during the winter of 1915/16 and perhaps had been mentioned by him in letters back from the front. The 9th Suffolks remained near Ypres until 5th April 1916, when they proceeded to Calais. Here, they remained in camp for ten days, "resting and thoroughly enjoying themselves" according to the Regimental History, before heading back to the Ypres salient.

Spells in the line alternated with periods of rest at the battalion's camp at Poperinghe behind the line, though "round about Ypres...the bombing and shelling of camps were the daily and nightly experiences of battalions supposedly at rest".

The Regimental History also records that on 3rd July 1916 the battalion marched to Bollezele, then on to Houtkerque "for the purposes of recuperation and training in open warfare", before heading back to billets in Ypres on 22nd July 1916[50].

By this time, the Battle of the Somme had begun. Originally, this had been planned as a mainly French offensive. However, the large German offensive at Verdun, which had begun on 21st February 1916 and was to last until 18th December that year, had diverted virtually all French manpower and efforts away from the Somme. Verdun was to cost an estimated 377,000 French and 337,000 German casualties[51].

The concentration of the French forces at Verdun meant the plan of attack for the Somme offensive evolved to become a mainly British assault.

On 1st July 1916, after eight days of heavy artillery bombardment, which had been expected to destroy the German defences, the main infantry attack went ahead, only to find the German defences had largely survived the barrage. Upon the artillery bombardment lifting to allow the infantry advance, the German soldiers swiftly re-emerged from deep bunkers to man their machine gun posts and fortifications, taking a huge toll of the British infantry. By the end of that day, the British Army had suffered over 57,000 casualties, of whom nearly 20,000 were dead: their largest ever loss in a single day[52]. Sixty per cent of all officers involved on the first day were killed[53].

Nonetheless, the Somme offensive continued into a second phase of battles from late July to the end of August 1916 and on towards a third phase in September.

At the beginning of August, the 9th Suffolks were withdrawn from the Ypres salient and moved to the Albert sector of the Somme, taking over trenches in front of Mailly-Maillet Wood on 5th August 1916 and remaining there till the 28th, except for a week behind the lines at Louvencourt. Whilst in the trenches at Mailly-Maillet Wood, "they were allotted the distressing task of clearing the battlefield of the fallen of the Ulster Division"[54]. These were bodies which had lain on the Somme battlefield since the main attack on 1st July.

After a further brief spell behind the lines, the battalion then moved back into trenches at Ginchy, from where, as part of the 6th Division, they attacked a heavily armed German position known as "the Quadrilateral" on the 13th September 1916, as part of the preparations for the Battle of Flers-Courcelette, which opened the third phase of the Somme campaign (*fig. 27*). The battalion war diary[55] describes the preliminary attack:

"13/9/16....Battalion were ordered to attack enemy's trenches. 'B' 'C' & 'D' Companies at 6.20am. 1st two lines of enemy's trenches were captured, but owing to heavy casualties from artillery and machine gun fire the situation could not be cleared up. At 7.30pm 'A' Company were ordered to attack the QUADRILATERAL but failed to reach their objective owing to very heavy machine gun fire. A new trench was dug by the battalion which enabled them to get in touch with the 2nd Sherwoods on the left and 8 Bedfords on the right. It also cleared up the situation. During these attacks the battalion behaved splendidly and it is regretted the casualties were heavy.
Killed Capt S H Byrne 2/Lieut. G.D.Gardner
Wounded 2/Lieut. C. Wayman 2/Lieut. A.G.Douglas Capt J. W. Barrett 2/Lieut. G.Collyer 2/Lieut. D.K.MacDonald 2/Lieut. H.E.Falkner 2/Lieut. A.Fudge 2/Lieut. F.Goatcher 2/Lieut. H.Almack Captain N.R.Rawson, R.A.M.C. attached 9th Suffolks
Killed other ranks 15 Wounded 185"

The main offensive began on the 15th September 1916, with the battle of Flers-Courcelette. This battle marked the first use of a new secret weapon invented by the British: the tank (*fig. 28*).

The objective of the 9th Suffolks on the 15th September lay beyond the Quadrilateral, the German position which they had been unsuccessful in attacking on the 13th. Therefore, they would now attack it again.

From the battalion war diary again[56]:

"The Brigade were ordered to attack the enemy's trenches and to push on to their final objective, which was between LESBOUCHS [sic: Lesboeufs] and MORVAL and to establish a line on the ridge.

The Brigade ordered the 1st Leicesters and 9th Norfolks to attack at 6.20am. The 2nd Sherwoods and 9th Suffolks were in support, the 9th Suffolks supporting 9th Norfolks. The battalion lined up to move forward at 7.50am. but owing to very heavy artillery and machine gun fire half of 'C' Company could not leave their trench.

The remainder of the battalion moved forward but were held up from heavy machine gun fire which came from the enemy's strong position called the QUADRILATERAL. It was from the machine guns that the battalion lost very heavily. Lieut. Col. A.P.Mack was killed at 8.30am. The remainder of battalion dug themselves in and got into touch with both flanks. The enemy's barrage was extremely heavy and caused many more casualties. The battalion held the line they established till relieved by the 14th Durham Light Infantry at 11pm and moved back to support trench where they reorganised.

Casualties were Killed Lieut. Col. A.P.Mack Lieut. J.T.C.Fallowes Lieut. L.A.Whillier 2/Lieut. F.Wilson and 35 other ranks

Wounded Capt L.E.Ensor [sic] Capt. S.W. CHURCH Lieut. J.N. Harmer 2/Lieut. W.H.HOILE 2/Lieut. C.G. GARDNER 2/ Lieut. G. Hopkins 2/Lieut. R.T.Scott and 99 other ranks Missing 2/ Lieut S.J.Price 2/Lieut. R.G.Smith and 93 other ranks"

In the course of the two attacks on 13th and 15th September 1916, the 9th Suffolks had incurred 452 casualties, about half their number, and still had not reached the Quadrilateral. As shown in the above entry, the wounded included Captain Lionel Ensor, the same officer who had written to Albert Last's parents to report their son's death.

Although the 9th Suffolks had suffered devastating casualties, a heavy toll had also been taken of the German defences and in a further attack two days later, on the 18th September 1916, the Quadrilateral was finally captured by the 1st Shropshire Light Infantry[57].

For the next day, 16th September, the war diary shows the battalion as 'in trenches', but no casualties are recorded. This is the date given for William Chenery to have been 'killed in action'[58], so it would seem more than likely that he was killed on the 15th September 1916, along with so many of his battalion, and that his death was only recorded when the next roll call took place on the 16th September. Similarly, the Commonwealth War Graves Commission shows 16th September 1916 as the date of death of 100 men of the 9th Battalion in total[59], many of whose bodies were never recovered from the battlefield and are listed amongst the names of the missing of the Somme on the Thiepval War Memorial.

The Somme campaign was finally brought to an end on 18th November 1916, with the first-day objective of Bapaume still six miles distant. British and French forces had advanced about six miles (9.7 km) on a front of sixteen miles (26 km), but at a combined cost of over 600,000 casualties[60]. German estimated casualty figures range from 500,000 to 680,000[61]

William Chenery junior is recorded on the the Thiepval Memorial to the missing (*fig. 29*). William's father William senior appears to have died in 1926[62] and his mother Eliza in 1939[63.]

SERGEANT HORACE WILLIAM SHERMAN

No. 3/593, 5th Battalion,
Duke of Edinburgh's (Wiltshire Regiment)
Died 1st February 1917, aged 38

Horace Sherman was born at Aspall, near Debenham, Suffolk, in 1878, the son of George Sherman, an agricultural labourer, and his wife Eliza (neé Pipe). He was the fourth or fifth of ten children, six boys and four girls.

In 1881, the family was at Aspall in Suffolk (*fig. 30*) and in 1891 at Brandeston (*fig. 31*). Horace, by now aged 12, is not shown as a scholar like his younger siblings, so had apparently left school by then.

By 1901, George had died and Eliza was living with four of her sons at Seven Gardens, Burgh, just a few doors away from young William Chenery[64]. However, Horace had already joined the Army five years earlier (*fig. 32*). In joining up, he gave his occupation as a ploughman, though he stated himself as already in the Medical Staff Militia (Eastern Countries). His Army service record also gives us a description of Horace (*fig. 33*).

In July 1898, the Ipswich Journal carried an account of an assault on him and a fellow soldier whilst stationed in Ipswich (*fig. 34*).

His Army service record shows Horace serving as a driver with the Royal Horse Artillery in India from late 1898 (*fig. 35*), before returning to Woolwich in England in 1910. Whilst serving, he received "G.C.", ie., good conduct pay, but three times this was forfeited, on one occasion for refusing to obey an order, on another occasion, the punishment included imprisonment with 14 days' hard labour. (*fig. 36*)

In 1911, Horace's widowed mother Eliza was still living at Burgh, with four sons[65]. Horace was now back in England, in barracks at Woolwich (fig. 37).

Horace's Army service record shows that he was discharged from 'H' Battery of the Royal Horse Artillery on 21st April 1914 (*fig. 38*). His obituary from the Wiltshire Times (*fig. 39*) states that he was employed at Blake's Brewery, Trowbridge, upon his discharge.

Horace married Kate Willcox in Wiltshire in mid-1914[66].

Upon the outbreak of war, Horace re-enlisted as a private with the 2nd Wiltshire Battalion. The battalion had crossed to Belgium on 7th October 1914, as part of the 21st Brigade of the 7th Division, and was soon in action in the Ypres sector, suffering heavy casualties at Reutel in late October 1914, which reduced the battalion to less than half its full strength[67].

Horace's medal card (*fig. 40*) shows a "qualifying date", which generally indicates the date he set foot on foreign soil, of 11th November 1914, so he would seem to have been part of the effort of bringing the 2nd Wiltshires back up to strength after their losses at Reutel.

From mid-November 1914, the battalion was in trenches near Fleurbaix, the battalion history recording the Christmas truce of 1914, which lasted until New Year's Eve. Following a very wet winter, they were eventually relieved by a battalion of Canadian troops on 2nd March 1915[68].

However, on 10th March 1915, it was back to the front line again, as the battalion took part in the Battle of Neuve Chappelle, near Bethune. Nearly 300 casualties were suffered, then over 150 more at the nearby Battle of Festubert in mid-May[69].

His *Wiltshire Times* obituary states that Horace was severely wounded on 23rd May 1915. However, the 2nd Wiltshires had been relieved and taken out of the front line on the 19th May[70], so it seems likely that Horace would have wounded on or before 19th May.

During his ensuing spell of leave in England, Horace's wife Kate became pregnant with their son, Horace Henry, who was born on 10th May 1916[71]. However, by the time Horace junior was born, his father had returned to active service, only this time in the Persian Gulf (*fig. 39*). The 5th Battalion of the Wiltshires had been in action there since February that year, as part of the 40th Brigade of the 13th (Western) Division[72], so it seems likely that Horace transferred from the 2nd Wiltshires (who remained on the Western Front) to the 5th Wiltshires, his final battalion, at this point.

On 18th April 1916, Horace was wounded again (*fig. 39*). At this time, his Division was positioned at Bait Isa in Mesopotamia, where British and Empire forces were attempting to break through Turkish defences in order to relieve the 6th (Poona) Division of the Indian Army, under Major-General Charles Townshend, who were being besieged by the Turks at Kut. After initially advancing at Bait Isa, the Division had been hit by a fierce Turkish counter-attack:

"The 4th South Wales Borderers and 5th Wiltshire (40th Brigade) arrived at the 8th Brigade position about 2 a.m. [on 18th April] and were sent to support the 59th Rifles. At 3 a.m. the Turks made

their fourth distinct attack on the 8th Brigade line, again directed mainly against the part of the line held by the 59th. Half an hour later the 47th Sikhs reported large enemy bodies massing to their front, and at 4 a.m. the Turks launched their fifth attack against the 8th Brigade, continuing to push in men in great vigour until it began to get light soon after 5 a.m. But, though in some cases they got quite close to the British line, they failed entirely to break the stout defence of the 8th Brigade, who had that night covered themselves with glory"[73]

The 5th Battalion's war diary for 18th April[74] shows:

"Mesopotamia, Beit Aiessa sic [Bait Isa] After heavy counter-attack 2 Lt S.C.R.L. Clark wounded, other ranks killed 11, wounded 47, missing 6."

Having been wounded again, his *Wiltshire Times* obituary (*fig. 39*) states that Horace was now sent to India to recuperate, before heading back to rejoin the British campaign in Mesopotamia.

The attempt to relieve the siege of Kut failed and Major-General Townshend finally surrendered along with about 13,000 men.

The fall of Kut was regarded as one of the most humiliating defeats in the history of the British Army[75] and efforts were soon put in hand to re-take the offensive against the Turks. A new commander, General Maude, was appointed, who carefully prepared his army for the new offensive. Obtaining reinforcements and more equipment, Maude directed his forces in a steady series of victories, advancing up the Tigris towards Baghdad.

On 25th January 1917, an attack began on what was known as the Hai salient. It was here that Horace Sherman was killed on 1st February 1917. The Battalion war diary for that date[76] shows:

"Mesopotamia, Moscow Trench - Moved up to ROME TRENCH via LONDON TRENCH to support the attack of the 8th Cheshire Regt. Good work was done by our bombers and line P10 F and P10 H was made good. Lieut & Adjutant R.I Scorer slightly wounded, remained with unit. Casualties O.R [other ranks] 1 Killed and 10 wounded. Relieved during night by the 8th BRIGADE and moved back to S9."

The Hai salient was soon captured, to complete another British victory under General Maude. Kut was re-taken in late February 1917 and, on 11th March, Baghdad was captured[77].

Horace Sherman has no recorded grave, but is listed on the Basra Memorial in Iraq (*fig. 41*). For political reasons, the Commonwealth War Graves Commission is unable to maintain the Basra Memorial at present, so those named on it are commemorated in a two volume Roll of Honour on display at the Commission's Head Office in Maidenhead, available for the public to view (*fig. 42*).

Horace Sherman appears to be the only one of the men listed on the Burgh War Memorial to have had any children. His son Horace Henry Sherman grew up to have several children and grandchildren of his own, making Horace senior also the only one of the men listed on the memorial to have living descendants.

GUNNER ROBERT BROOM

No. 116131, 252nd Siege Battery,
Died 25th April 1918, aged 28

Robert Broom was born at Burgh in 1889, the son of George Broom, an agricultural labourer, and his wife Emma (neé Dunnett)[78]. He was one of thirteen children.

In 1891, the family was living at "The Mount", Burgh (near the church)(*fig. 43*). In 1901, the family was at Otley Road, Burgh, which may perhaps be the same address as in 1891 (*fig. 44*).

In 1911, only Robert of all the children appears still to have lived with his parents. They were now living at Mill Cottage, Burgh (*fig. 45*). Eleven of the children are recorded as surviving, so the other ten had either moved out or were just not at home on census night.

Young Robert is shown as a labourer.

On enlisting in the Army in February 1916, he gave his occupation as being a shepherd (*fig. 46*). He gave his father, George, as his next of kin (*fig. 47*). His medical examination (*fig. 48*), in checking his eyesight, records that "probably can see better when he has not had so much Beer [*sic*]", suggesting some "Dutch courage" may have played a part in Robert's enlistment.

On joining up, Robert was posted to the 252nd Siege Battery, Royal Garrison Artillery, which he joined in September 1916. (*fig. 49*). The battery arrived in France on 3rd February 1917[79]. The battery consisted of 6 six-inch siege howitzers[80] and would have been used to provide heavy artillery support in the field.

Judging by the locations of the graves of those soldiers of the 252nd battery killed in the war[81], the battery was based in the Ypres sector until at least mid-1918 (*fig. 50*).

In February 1918, Robert's father, George, died at the age of 70. The records do not indicate whether the news of his father's death would have reached Robert on the Western Front in the following days and weeks.

Robert himself then died on 25th April 1918, which date coincides with a major German offensive at Mount Kemmel, south of Ypres, part of the Battle of the Lys (also known as the Lys Offensive, the Fourth Battle of Ypres, the Fourth Battle of Flanders and Operation Georgette) (*fig. 51*), part of the German Spring Offensive. This was a German effort to win the war quickly, before America's entry into the war in 1917 could prove decisive. The German forces on the Western Front had also been supplemented by forces freed from the Eastern

Front following their armistice with Russia in December 1917.

The Michelin Illustrated Guides To The Battlefields (1914—1918): Ypres And The Battles Of Ypres[82] gives the following details:

The Capture of Kemmel Hill
(April 22-28, 1918.)

A period of comparative calm followed, during which the Germans prepared a fresh mass attack, in view of the capture of the Hills.

...At 2.30 a.m. on April 25 the attack began with a heavy bombardment, in which the proportion of gas shells was far greater than previously.

At about 6 a.m. the infantry assault began in a dense fog north and south of Kemmel Hill. North of the Hills the "Sieger" divisions, marching west to east, had orders to capture Kemmel Village, and then, via the Valley of the Kemmelbeek, join up at Locre with the Eberhardt Divisions, which were attacking from north to south in the direction of Dranoutre.

On the left of the attacking front, the village of Kemmel was taken by the Germans, in spite of a heroic defence. Step by step the British 9th Division was driven back into Kemmelbeek valley and on Dickebusch Pond.

In the centre the enemy storm-troop waves, after several repulses, finally reached the summit of Kemmel Hill, where a fierce hand-to-hand encounter took place. In spite of their great heroism, the 30th Infantry Regiment, outnumbered and almost surrounded, was forced to abandon the position, but only after a dashing counter-attack by a battalion of the 99th Infantry had failed to extricate them. On the right, the German Alpine Corps, by a daring manœuvre, made possible by the fog and the broken nature of the ground, succeeded in reaching the artillery positions, which were at once attacked by machine-gun fire. The French and British batteries, under a storm of bullets, were obliged to retreat, saving what material they could and blowing up the rest.

The Germans thus reached the village of Locre, which changed hands several times during the day.

Finally, after a counter-attack, the 154th Infantry Division remained masters of the village, although the Germans succeeded in holding the "hospice" at the southern end.

The situation was now critical and the enemy advance had to be checked at all costs. On the night of the 25th the Allies were reinforced by the 39th Infantry Division (Massenet) at the very moment a fresh German offensive was being launched. The timely arrival of these troops effectually stayed the German thrust.

On the evening of the 26th, after much sanguinary fighting, the enemy paused, exhausted. The French took advantage of the respite to consolidate new positions.

Perhaps Robert was wounded in the German artillery bombardment preceding the attack on Mount Kemmel or in the infantry attack which followed. What we do know is that he is recorded as wounded on 25th April 1918 and having died the following day at "64 C.C.S", meaning 64 Casualty Clearing Station (*fig. 49*), which was positioned near Proven, a village north-west of Ypres. A total of 13 soldiers of the 252nd Siege Battery are shown on the Commonwealth War Graves Commission website as having died on 25th April 1918[83].

Robert is buried at the Mendinghem Cemetery, Poperinge, near Ypres (*fig. 52*). The cemetery name was actually invented by the troops during the War for the nearby Casualty Clearing Stations, to mimic Flemish place-names - as well as Mendinghem, 'mending 'em', there were also 'Bandaghem' and 'Dozinghem' stations, all three now perpetuated by the names of the cemeteries they gave rise to.

Robert's death meant that his mother had suffered the loss of her husband and a son within just over two months of each other.

On 24th May 1918, Robert's family and fianceé Edie placed a memorial of him in the local newspaper, the Suffolk Chronicle and Mercury (*fig. 53*).

Robert's mother Emma died in 1923 and is buried with his father in the churchyard at Burgh (*fig. 54*).

Their gravestone at Burgh churchyard carries the following inscription in memory of Robert.

In Loving Memory of

ROBERT BROOM

THEIR THIRD BELOVED SON

DIED OF WOUNDS IN FRANCE

APRIL 25, 1918 AGED 27

[nb. Robert's birth registration and census records show him to have been 28 or 29 at his death]

CHAPTER 2

THE END OF THE WAR

The German offensive at the Lys ground to a halt by the end of April 1918 and further German offensives were repulsed between April and July 1918, leaving the German forces seriously depleted and facing Allied forces that had been reinforced by over a million American troops and additional British troops released from the campaigns in Italy and Palestine.

The initiative in the War now passed rapidly to the Allies and, in August 1918, a series of Allied attacks, which became known as the Hundred Days Offensive, decisively drove the Germans back, leading to the signing of the Armistice at 11am on 11 November 1918.

The rapid defeat of the German forces, just months after being on the offensive, would soon come to be attributed to the betrayal of the German Army by the lack of civilian support on the home front – the 'stab in the back' – for which Germany's Jews and Communists would bear the brunt of the blame.

In addition, the Treaty of Versailles, which formally ended the War and which was signed on 28 June 1919, imposed harsh reparation terms on Germany:

> "It cannot be denied that the conditions were somewhat draconian. Germany accepted responsibility for the war and lost 68,000 km² of territory, including Alsace and Lorraine, which had been annexed in 1870, and 8 million inhabitants. Part of western Prussia was given to Poland, which gained access to the sea through the famous "Polish Corridor", and Germany agreed to pay the crushing sum of 20 billion gold marks in reparations claimed by France. In addition, it lost most of its ore and agricultural production. Its colonies were confiscated, and its military strength was crippled. Humiliated, Germany seethed for revenge. A new war, which everyone had hoped to avoid, was already blowing up on the horizon almost as soon as the German delegation receded over it."[84]

So, the scene was set for the descent towards the Second World War.

CHAPTER 3

TWO FURTHER CASUALTIES
ASSOCIATED WITH BURGH

The Commonwealth War Graves Commission records two further casualties[85] of the Great War associated with Burgh, with the following information:

PRIVATE DANIEL WHAYMAN BEDINGFIELD

6379, 13th Bn., Middlesex Regiment, died 16 April 1917
Age at death: 41

Cemetery: Lievin Communal Cemetery Extension, Pas de Calais, France
Grave Reference: I. C. 14.

Additional Information: Son of John and Mary Bedingfield, late of Burgh; husband of Bloomfield Bedingfield, of Boot St., Great Bealings, Woodbridge, Suffolk.

RIFLEMAN LIONEL SIDNEY GEORGE BUCKMAN

(listed as L.S.G. Buckman), 321670, 6th Bn., London Regiment (City of London Rifles), died 7 April 1918 [aged 24]

Grave Reference: II. F. 28.
Cemetery: Abbeville Communal Cemetery Extension, Somme, France

Additional Information: Son of Mrs. Buckman, of Burgh, Woodbridge, Suffolk.

CHAPTER 4

THE DEDICATION OF THE WAR MEMORIAL

Historic England, the public body that looks after England's historic environment, records that "the absence of the British Empire's 1.1 million dead created a powerful need for monuments. No greater wave of public remembrance has ever happened in history.... tens of thousands of war memorials were erected"[86].

The war memorial at Burgh was dedicated relatively soon after the war, on 28th September 1919, being only the second memorial to be dedicated in Suffolk.

The East Anglian Daily Times of Monday, 29th September 1919[87], contains a description of the memorial and dedication ceremony, as follows:

TO BURGH HEROES
A SUFFOLK VILLAGE
MEMORIAL.

There were many quiet and charming spots in the Suffolk country which in war days gave gallant London lads, whose after deeds became imperishable, a new and interesting phase to all they read of East Anglia. Such a one was Burgh, on the fringes of what the well-known 58th Division would call the Woodbridge country. Some of these lads, like the country community itself, would have been touched by the impressiveness of a ceremony figured there on Sunday afternoon. Burgh lads donned khaki – a fine contribution of no less than 49 in a population which numbers just over a couple of hundred. Five made the supreme sacrifice, and the ceremony was the unveiling of a memorial, taking the shape of a granite cross, which now dominates in a commanding position on the bank above the fork of the road approached by those coming from Ipswich. It stands beneath the shadow of the old church, which has its interior religiously dimmed with memorial windows on all of its four sides. The little church had its pews uncomfortably filled for the service, and it was fitting in more ways than one that the practically new Rector should be officiating, for his acquaintance is with Suffolk and France. After association with several churches in the county, the Rev G M Shallard went a few years ago to take the British chaplaincy at Rouen. He was there when the war came, and could relate many experiences of a French town so reminiscent to Tommy of a famous "bull ring". A sympathetic note sounded through the service, which began in the church with choral effects, the village choir leading familiar hymns. The Rev Canon Page, D.D., C.F., rector of the adjoining parish church at Clopton, who, curiously enough, was also at the Rouen Base during his last two years of service, spoke from the pulpit. His words commanded attention in the sympathy of their strain and worthiness of intent.

"The way of Britain's welfare is the way of unity and mutual help", he declared. "Every time you pass that memorial remind yourselves of those who have gone before. They expect something from you; not mere words of pride, but a living worthy of their great sacrifice and seeking to do your part in making glad for all life in a land which they helped to save."

The Canon was speaking to the fitting text, "Their name liveth for evermore." It was, he commented, in very loving memory of their dear brave ones that they had put up that memorial, and the form of the memorial seemed to speak the way they had gone, the way of sacrifice, hardship, suffering, the way of all noble living, for the life which knew nothing of the Cross, of self-sacrifice, and living for others, that life was a worthless and ignoble one. The Cross was the symbol of victory. They erected it in proud memory of those named amongst the saviours of their country. Patriots they were, if ever such men lived, and it was for them not merely to be proud, but worthy of them. "Perhaps England" observed Canon Page, "has a harder task ahead than even in the anxious days of war, and our task, if it be worthy of of those who laid down their lives for us, is to build up an England that shall be worthy of their sacrifice. Cannot we, who banded together in those dark days, stand shoulder to shoulder and help each other through the days that lie in front of us?". The call of to-day to the nation was that we should learn to follow Christ, cultivate His spirit of self-sacrifice and kindness, then would happy days be ours again.

The folk filed out of the church in procession when service was over, and gathered round the memorial, with the Boy Scouts immediately facing it, one of the fallen having been of their number. First Canon Page dedicated the piece of ground, for it lies just outside the churchyard; and then unveiling the granite emblem, he dedicated that also. Inscribed on the front of it could be read the words: "To the glory of God and in loving memory of Robert Broom, R.G.A.; Wm. C. Chenery, 2nd Su olks; Herbert C. Hughes, 2nd Black Watch; Alfred [sic] Victor Last, 2nd [sic] Suffolks, Horace Sherman, R.H.A.; Lest we forget." Many floral tributes were laid at the foot of the memorial as the assembly sang "Peace, perfect peace."

The former church schoolroom in the village, now used for parish meetings and events, contains a photograph of the dedication ceremony (*fig. 55*), with the following text: "The dedication of Burgh war memorial on 28 September 1919. This photograph shows Canon Page (Rector of Clopton), the Rev G M Shallard (Rector of Burgh), Mark Barlow of Hasketon (who donated the land) and Captain Sutton Smith, as well as the families of the five men killed in the War and named on the memorial".

CHAPTER 5

THE GREAT WAR ROLL OF HONOUR

The Roll of Honour inside Burgh parish church gives the names of a further forty-three men of the village who served in the war and survived. Seven of these are listed as "formerly resident in this parish".

To give an idea of the proportion of the young men of the village who joined up, the 1911 census for Burgh lists forty-eight males aged between 8 and 30 as present in the parish on census night. Of these, twenty-five are listed on the Roll of Honour, suggesting that about half of the males of the village who would have been aged between 15 and 33 at some point during the war in fact joined up. This must have had a very significant effect on the life of the village during the war.

The Roll of Honour, listing the servicemen and their regiments, is set out as follows:

R.J. ABLITT R.G.A

S. ABLITT R.F.A

T.W.ABLITT R.G.A

DANIEL ABLITT 2ND SUFF.

DANIEL ABLITT 5TH MIDDX

STANLEY BAXTER R.F.A

SIDNEY BAXTER 2ND

LIFEGUARDS

H.BROOM R.F.A

W.BROOM R.MAR.A.

C.BRUNDELL R.G.A

W.G. CHENERY 1ST

F.W. FRIEND QUEEN'S

C. CRACKNELL R.N.

W.R. CRANE M.G.C.

W. CRANE R.G.A

A. FAIRS R.G.A.A

L. FRIEND R.E

H. FRIEND R.A.M.C.

M.FRIEND R.N.

C.E. FRIEND R.G.A.

G.E. HEATH R.F.A.

A.E. HUGHES R.F.A.

H.G. HUGHES 2nd BLACK WATCH

J.H. HUGHES CAN INFY

F.J. HUGHES K.R.R.

H.W.OSBORN R.MAR.A

H.GRAY R.E.

C.F. HUGHES 9TH SUFF

H. KIDBY ROYAL IRISH RIFLES

E. LAST RIFLE BRIGADE

S. LAST 2ND WELSH REGT

H. LAST 2ND WELSH REGT

A. LAST 9TH SUFF.

L. LAST R.E.

H. MANN 3RD ESSEX

W. NOBLE 2ND LIFE GUARDS

E.E. ROSE R.G.A.

SUTTON SMITH COMDR.R.N.

W.C. WOOD 8TH SUFF.

A. SHERMAN

ALSO FORMERLY RESIDENT IN THIS PARISH

C.W. BELL

G.CHAPMAN 2ND SUFF.

C. KING R.E.

H.W. OSBORN R.MAR.A

C.F. OSBORN R.G.A.

A. SHERMAN R.G.A

R. SHERMAN R.G.A.

H SHERMAN R.H.A.

H. SMY R.INNIS.FUS.

CHAPTER 6

THE SECOND WORLD WAR

Estimates of German casualty figures in the Great War vary, but tend to range from 1.5 to 2.5 million dead across all theatres of the war, out of a population in 1910 of about 65 million, so roughly between 2 to 4 per cent of the population. These losses at least match British losses as a proportion of the population and yet we know that Germany was willing to risk going to war against Britain and France again little more than twenty years later. The reasons for this are generally cited as feelings of betrayal at the outcome of the Great War, blamed in part upon Germany's Jewish population, resentment towards the terms of the peace forced upon them via the Treaty of Versailles (see Chapter Two above) and a belief in the need for lebensräum or 'living space' for the German people, including securing natural resources beyond Germany's existing boundaries. All of these views were more or less represented in the person of Adolf Hitler, himself a veteran of the Great War, and through his National Socialist party, which swept to power in Germany in 1933.

Whatever the reasons behind the outbreak of the Second World War, it is clear that German expansionism was strong enough to overcome all objections based on her experience of the Great War. After the annexation of Austria and Czechoslovakia in 1938, the German invasion of Poland in September 1939 finally saw the outbreak of war with Britain and France.

The war was to take a very different course from the Great War. Poland fell quickly in 1939, to be followed by Denmark, Norway, Luxembourg, Belgium, the Netherlands and France between April and June 1940. There were to be no static lines of trenches this time around, as the mobility of Germany's mechanised forces forced the French and British forces back to the French coast before any solid line of defence could be put in place. With the fall of Dunkirk on 4th June 1940, Britain and its empire stood alone and largely able to wage war against Germany and its Axis partner Italy only in the skies, at sea and in North Africa.

Britain remained alone until the German invasion of Russia in June 1941 brought the Russians into the war as allies. This was followed by the Japanese attack on Pearl Harbour in December that year, which saw Japan join the Axis forces and the United States enter the war as allies with the British and Russian forces. Japan immediately launched offensives against British possessions in Burma and Malaysia and took Singapore in February 1942.

The war now began to turn decisively the way of the Allies. The Russians first stopped the German advance eastwards in front of Moscow at the end of 1941. The Americans then inflicted a devastating defeat on Japan at the Battle of Midway in June 1942. For Britain, victory in the Battle of El Alamein in November 1942 proved the beginning of the end for the German North African campaign.

At sea, the U-boat war would remain in the balance heading into 1943, but increasing German submarine losses forced U-boat attacks to be scaled back from May that year.

In the air, Britain began to launch massive bomber raids against German cities, including the first 'thousand-bomber' raid against Cologne in May 1942.

In September 1943, the Allies gained their first foothold upon continental Europe with the invasion of Italy, to be followed by the D-Day Normandy landings on 6th June 1944.

On the Eastern front, the Russians defeated the German Sixth Army at Stalingrad in February 1943 and lifted the siege of Leningrad (now St Petersburg) in January 1944.

With the fall of Berlin on 8th May 1945, the war in Europe was over.

The Japanese surrendered on 15th August 1945, following the American destruction by atomic bombs of the Japanese cities of Hiroshima and Nagasaki, bringing the global conflict to an end.

Burgh's war memorial lists three men who fell in the Second World War. One died in the North African campaign, one on a bomber raid over Germany and the last in a Japanese prisoner of war camp.

The memorial carries the following inscription:

1939 - 1945 Lest we forget

HARRY PATERNOSTER SUFF.

ARTHUR WOODS SUFF.

DESMOND YOUNGS R.A.F.

The details of Second World War servicemen can be more difficult to find than those of Great War servicemen: service records are not generally available and the census returns from 1921 and later have not been published as yet, due to the rule that census data not be published for 100 years.

Nonetheless, some details have been found and these follow.

CHAPTER 7

LEST WE FORGET:
THREE MORE MEN OF BURGH
Burgh's Second World War Fallen

PRIVATE HARRY PATERNOSTER

No. 5827448, Suffolk Regiment
Died 6th April 1941, aged 19

The Second World War

Harry Paternoster was born in 1921, the son of Herbert and Jeanie Paternoster of Burgh[88]. He appears to have had an older sister, Daisy[89] (later Daisy Swann[90]), who died in 1997[91] and an older brother, Allan[92], who died in 1994[93].

Harry was a private in the Suffolk Regiment (No. 5827448), but was attached to A Battalion, No. 7 Commando[94], which means he volunteered for 'Special Service of a Hazardous Nature'.

No. 7 Commando was raised from regiments based in the eastern counties of England throughout the summer of 1940 and the unit mustered at Felixstowe in July 1940[95].

Harry Paternoster's Commando battalion transferred to the Middle East in January 1941 and was placed within "Layforce", a brigade of the British 6th Division, attached to the 8th Army[96]. Layforce was named after its commander, Colonel Robert Laycock, and would go on to carry out raids on Axis positions in the Mediterranean and Middle Eastern theatres.

However, Harry Paternoster appears to have been No. 7 Commando's first casualty of the War, dying of heatstroke on Sunday, 6th April 1941[97], at 13th General Hospital, Suez.

Private Harry Paternoster is buried in the Ismailia War Memorial Cemetery in Egypt[98] (*figs. 56 and 57*). The inscription on his headstone reads:

"TWAS BETTER THAT WE LOSE HIM
THAN FOR HIM TO SUFFER PAIN

WE HOPE THAT OUR GREAT
LOSS IS HIS ETERNAL GAIN"

SERGEANT DESMOND CLAUDE YOUNGS

Air Gunner, No 1874065, Squadron 5,
Group 57, Royal Air Force
Died 24th March 1944, aged 20

Desmond Youngs was born in 1923, the son of Claude and Emma Elizabeth Youngs[99]. He appears to have had two older brothers, Sidney and Norman[100, 101].

Desmond's father Claude's address at the time of administering Desmond's estate in 1945 was given as Moat Farm, Burgh, and his occupation as a farmer[102]. Desmond's mother Emma had died in 1943[103].

Desmond served as a sergeant in the Royal Air Force Volunteer Reserve and flew as an air gunner with 57 Squadron[104], operating from the bomber airfield at East Kirkby in Lincolnshire.

On the night of 24th March 1944, Desmond took part in a bombing raid on Berlin, as the rear gunner in Avro Lancaster ND671. Though this was not a "thousand bomber raid", nonetheless it was still a very substantial attack, involving 811 aircraft[105].

Lancaster ND671, with Desmond Youngs as tail gunner, took off from East Kirkby at 1850 hours.

The crew of the Lancaster were:

> *RAAF 415527 PO Hampton, G A Captain (Pilot)*
> *RAF Sgt F S Bodkin, (Flight Engineer)*
> *RAF Sgt R E G Nuttall (Navigator)*
> *RCAF Flt Sgt T J Adkison, (Air Bomber)*
> *RAF Sgt J Milfull, (Wireless Air Gunner)*
> *RCAF PO Strom, C A (Mid Upper Gunner)*
> *RAF Sgt D C Youngs, (Rear Gunner)*

Nothing was heard from the aircraft after take off and it failed to return to base. The Lancaster appears to have made it to the target, but when homebound at 21,000 feet, it was shot down by flak and crashed near Geseke, a large town near Lippstadt, Germany. Five of the crew, including Desmond Youngs, were killed. Sergeants Nuttall and Milfull became prisoners of war[106]. Sergeant Nuttall was confined in Hospital due to his injuries. Sergeant Milfull was interned in Camps L6/357, PoW No.3399[107].

The five men who died, including Desmond Youngs, were originally buried at Geseke Cemetery, Germany (*fig. 61*), but were moved to Hanover War Cemetery[108] in 1947 (*fig. 58*).

The headstone for Desmond Youngs carries the following inscription:

"TO US WHO LOVED AND LOST YOU,
DEAR TO OUR HEARTS YOU WILL ALWAYS REMAIN"

The raid of 24/25th March proved costly for Bomber Command. The bomber stream was scattered on its way to the target by high winds and many of the bombers that reached Berlin appear to have missed the main target areas within the city. German anti-aircraft guns and nightfighters then took a heavy toll on the aircraft returning home. Seventy-two aircraft were lost, along with 392 men killed and 131 taken prisoners of war. Nonetheless, approximately 2,500 tons of bombs were dropped in the Berlin area in the raid.

This was to turn out to be the last raid in the "Battle of Berlin", a bombing offensive against the German capital which had begun in August 1943 and totalled nineteen major raids. However, the bombing campaign against Berlin also proved costly in terms of aircraft and aircrew casualties, costing seven per cent of Bomber Command's total wartime aircraft losses.

After the raid in March 1944, attention switched to preparations for the D-Day landings in Normandy and there were to be no further major raids on Berlin before the war ended[109].

GRAVES CONCENTRATION REPORT FORM

Copy to...

Report No. BAOR/GR/CON/1021

Germany 697E. 466.

(3½ m. W. of CENTRE of HANNOVER).

The following has / have been concentrated here:—

Name (Cemetery) — HANNOVER (LIMMER) British Cemetery

(Full Map Reference) — GSGS 4346 1/250,000 Sht L 53 X 306220

(1) Serial No.	(2) Regt or Corps	(3) Army No.	(4) Name & Initials	(5) Rank	(6) Date of Death	(7) K/A, D/W or Died	(8) Plot	(9) Row	(10) Grave	(11) Date of Reburial	Previous location of grave — Place & Map Ref.	Report Number
1	R.A.A.F.	Aus. 4082?? N.R.	HAMPTON G.A	P/O	24.3.44	K/A	XV	K	1	9.12.47	Plot 8 Grave 1	
2	R.A.F.	1874065	YOUNGS D.C	SGT	"	"	XV	K	2	"	8 3	
3	R.C.A.F.	R.194343 N.R.	STROM C.W	SGT	"	"	XV	K	3	"	8 4	
4	R.A.F.	1222687 N.R.	BODKIN F.S	SGT	"	"	XV	K	4	"	8 2	
5	R.A.F.	R.76149 N.R.	ADKISON / ATKINSON A.W.J	F/SGT	"	"	XV	K	5	"	8 5	E/27035
6											GESEKE, Cemetery, Germany.	
7											Germany.	
8											GSGS 4416 1/100,000	
9											Sht Q 3, 535385	
10												
11												
12												

Duplicate returned 15/12/48

Date: 7 January 48

Signed...

Rank & Appointment... A/Lt Col... ADJ GR

* Where a grave has not already been registered, a Registration Return on A.F.W. 3372 will

fig 61. Graves Concentration Report Form showing burial of Desmond Youngs and the other crew of Lancaster ND671 at Geseke and Hanover Cemeteries

PRIVATE ARTHUR HENRY WOODS

No. 5834445, 4th Battalion, Suffolk Regiment
Died 28th January 1945, aged 37

The Second World War

Arthur Henry Woods appears to have been born at Henley, Suffolk, in 1907, the son of Elijah and Minnie Woods[110]. Certainly, Elijah and Minnie, with their children, Ernest, Ethel, Frederick, and three year old son Arthur, were living at Henley in the 1911 census[111].

In 1940, Arthur married Flora Last[112] who was from Grundisburgh[113] (perhaps related to Albert Last), and the couple lived at Number 3, Seven Gardens, Burgh[114].

Arthur joined the Army as a private in the 4th Battalion of the Suffolk Regiment[115]. Both his battalion and the 5th Battalion of the Suffolk Regiment were shipped to Singapore in late January 1942, as part of the 18th Division of the British Army[116].

The 4th Battalion was almost immediately sent into action against Japanese forces advancing on Singapore. The Battalion suffered heavy casualties, only to be forced to surrender to the Japanese with the fall of Singapore on 15th February 1942[117]. Winston Churchill, called it the "worst disaster" in British military history, with about 80,000 British, Indian and Australian troops captured[118].

Following their capture, the men of the 18th Division were initially held at the Changi prison camp near Singapore[119], being used as forced labour around Singapore. From mid-1942 onwards, however, the Japanese began to disperse the men to various destinations, including a large number who were sent to work on the Burma railway[120]. However, many men were also sent by transport ship to Taiwan (then known as Formosa), to work as forced labour there, and their numbers included Arthur Woods, who was shipped out of Singapore in October 1942, arriving in Taiwan in November 1942[121].

The terrible treatment that the prisoners of war received on board the Japanese transport ships led to the ships becoming known as "hellships". Arthur Woods appears to have been transported to Taiwan on board one of three hellships to have reached Taiwan from Singapore in November 1942, the *England Maru*, the *Dainichi Maru* or the *Singapore Maru*[122].

Conditions on board the *England Maru* were described by another prisoner, Arthur Titherington:

"It was during this voyage I really learned to overcome any squeamishness I might still have had. With my shoulder against

a bulkhead, and one leg braced against an upright to counter the rolling of the ship, I sat eating one of our twice daily portions of boiled rice, while at the same time watching a man who was obviously in the throes of dysentery.

With his backside on a latrine bucket he was vomiting from his other end into a container, and quite often missing it. With the next roll of the ship he pitched forward, spilling the contents of both containers, and went crashing down on the deck. I put down my rice, wiped up the spillage as best as I could, helped him back onto the bucket and returned to my meal. My sensibilities had been brought to a point of complete numbness."[123]

Upon reaching Taiwan, Arthur was then based at Taichu and Kinkaseki camps for the next two years[124].

The prisoners at Taichu camp were engaged in a huge river reconstruction project and subjected to hours of hard labour in the hot tropical sun[125].

Moving to Kinkaseki camp, Arthur worked as forced labour in the nearby copper mine. The prisoners at Kinkaseki suffered terribly at the hands of the Japanese.

"[The mine] was so hot and dangerous that the local Taiwanese and Japanese miners refused to go there. If the men did not meet the quota of work set out for them at the beginning of the day.... they were lined up along the walls of the mine shaft and beaten with the hardwood handles of the mining hammers until they were black and blue with bruises and bleeding....the food was insufficient and this led to many types of diseases resulting from lack of food and vitamins. Dysentery, pellagra, beri beri, ulcers, pneumonia, diptheria and many other ailments took their toll on the men. Add to this the lack of medicines - and those that were available were often withheld by the Japanese, so that the doctors in the camp had a very hard time trying to keep the men alive. Many men died in the camp and when others became too sick and weak to work in the mine any longer, they were moved out to other camps"[126].

Arthur appears to have been moved out of the Kinkaseki camp to the Shirakawa camp, near Kagi on Taiwan, on 25th October 1944[127.] The Shirakawa camp appears to have been used mainly as a hospital by this time[128], so it would seem likely that Arthur had become gravely ill from his ordeal.

Arthur Woods died at the Shirakawa camp on 28th January 1945[129], being buried at the nearby Kozan cemetery[130]. A diary kept by Lieutenant Quartermaster (later Captain) James William Hugo of the 155th Field Regiment, Royal Artillery, a British officer also captured at Singapore, records Arthur's death:

> *"28th Jan/45 - Sunday, rest day. My 54th Birthday. I sincerely hope that my next one will be at home with Gracie and the boys. Another lad named Woods died today"*[131.]

Although Arthur was originally buried in Taiwan, his remains, as with the known remains of all those who died as prisoners in Taiwan, were moved to Hong Kong and re-buried in Sai Wan War Cemetery there in 1946[132] (*figs. 59 and 60*).

Arthur's parents, Elijah and Minnie, both died in the late 1940's[133,] [134]. His wife, Flora, remarried in 1951, to Ralph Banthorpe[135]. Flora died locally in 1994[136] and Ralph in 2000[137].

CHAPTER 8

A FURTHER CASUALTY OF
THE SECOND WORLD WAR
ASSOCIATED WITH BURGH

The Commonwealth War Graves Commission records one further casualty[138] of the Second World War associated with Burgh, with the following information:

SARAH JANE SMITH

(Civilian), died 16 September 1940
Age at death: 71

Reporting Authority: Lewisham, Metropolitan Borough
Additional Information: of 43 C London Road.

Daughter of the late Daniel and Sarah Baxter, of
Burgh, Suffolk; widow of William Smith.
Died at 41 C London Road.

CHAPTER 9

THE SECOND WORLD WAR ROLL OF HONOUR

Burgh Church also contains a Roll of Honour listing the men of the village who served in the Second World War (see opposite).

The Roll lists twenty three men, including the three men killed in the war and listed on the village war memorial. This compares with forty men listed on the Roll of Honour from the First World War (see page 113 above), so just more than half the number. The population of Burgh seems to have fluctuated slightly, but to have remained roughly around the 200 mark between the two wars[139]. Therefore, a substantially lower proportion of the male population of the village seems to have become military personnel in the Second World War, which presumably reflects the fact that, as previously mentioned, there was no repeat of the trench war stalemate that had so dominated the Western Front in the Great War.

ON SERVICE AGAINST EVIL
for FAITH AND FREEDOM

THE MEN OF OUR PARISH

ARTHUR BENNETT	SIGNALS
CHARLES CATTERMOLE	SUFFOLKS
GEORGE CATTERMOLE	SUFFOLKS
PETER CATTERMOLE	R.A.F.
ALBERT COTTON	2ND CAMBS.
FRANK GOULD	R.A.F.
ARTHUR LAMBERT	R.A.
JOHN LAMBERT	PIONEERS
PERCY LANKESTER	R.A.F.
MELLIS LAST	QUEEN'S
THOMAS LAST	R.A.
LEONARD MANN	R.A.S.C.
ALLEN PATERNOSTER	SUFFOLKS
HARRY PATERNOSTER	SUFFOLKS *Died on Service*
REGINALD SWAN	R.A.
JACK THORPE	R.A.S.C.
KENNETH TITSHALL	R.A.F.
ARTHUR WOODS	SUFFOLKS *Died Prisoner of War*
NORMAN YOUNGS	R.A.
DESMOND YOUNGS	R.A.F. *Killed in Action*
WALTER LAMBERT	SOMERSET LIGHT INFANTRY
MAURICE LAMBERT	LEICESTERSHIRE REGT.
ROBERT LAST	R.A.F.

"WITH THE CROSS OF JESUS, GOING ON BEFORE."
"LEST WE FORGET."

Abbreviations: Signals: Royal Corps of Signals. Suffolks: Suffolk Regiment, R.A.F: Royal Air Force, 2nd Cambs: 2nd Battalion The Cambridgeshire Regimen (Territorial Army), R.A: Royal Artillery, Pioneers: Pioneer Corps, Queen's: Queen's Royal Regiment (West Surrey)

This work is based on data provided through *www.VisionofBritain.org.uk* and uses historical material which is copyright of the Great Britain Historical GIS Project and the University of Portsmouth

The following references have been used and obtained from the source given for each:

1881 census: [database on-line]. *Ancestry.com*, Provo, UT, USA: Ancestry.com Operations Inc, 2004. 1881 British Isles Census Index provided by The Church of Jesus Christ of Latter-day Saints © Copyright 1999 Intellectual Reserve, Inc. All rights reserved. Original data: Census Returns of England and Wales, 1881. Kew, Surrey, England: The National Archives of the UK (TNA): Public Record Office (PRO), 1881. Images © Crown copyright. Images reproduced by courtesy of The National Archives, London, England.

1891 census: [database on-line]. *Ancestry.com*, Provo, UT, USA: Ancestry.com Operations Inc, 2005. Original data: Census Returns of England and Wales, 1891. Kew, Surrey, England: The National Archives of the UK (TNA): Public Record Office (PRO), 1891.

1901 census: [database on-line]. *Ancestry.com*, Provo, UT, USA: Ancestry.com Operations Inc, 2005. Original data: Census Returns of England and Wales, 1901. Kew, Surrey, England: The National Archives, 1901.

1911 census: [database on-line]. *Ancestry.com*, Provo, UT, USA: *Ancestry.com* Operations, Inc., 2011. Original data: Census Returns of England and Wales, 1911. Kew, Surrey, England: The National Archives of the UK (TNA), 1911.

Birth Index, 1916-2005 [database on-line]. *Ancestry.com*, Provo, UT, USA: Ancestry.com Operations Inc, 2008. Original data: General Register Office. England and Wales Civil Registration Indexes. London, England: General Register Office. © Crown copyright.

Free BMD births [database on-line]. *Ancestry.com*, Provo, UT, USA: Ancestry.com Operations Inc, 2006. Original data: General Register Office. England and Wales Civil Registration Indexes. London, England: General Register Office. © Crown copyright. Published by permission of the Controller of HMSO and the Office for National Statistics.

England & Wales, Marriage Index, 1916-2005 [database on-line]. *Ancestry.com*, Provo, UT, USA: Ancestry.com Operations, Inc, 2010. Original data: General Register Office. England and Wales Civil Registration Indexes. London, England: General Register Office. © Crown copyright.

Free BMD marriages: [database on-line]. *Ancestry.com*, Provo, UT, USA: Ancestry.com Operations Inc, 2006.

Original data: General Register Office. England and Wales Civil Registration Indexes. London, England: General Register Office. © Crown copyright. Published by permission of the Controller of HMSO and the Office for National Statistics.

Deaths: [database on-line]. *Ancestry.com*, Provo, UT, USA: Ancestry.com Operations Inc, 2007. Original data: General Register Office. England and Wales Civil Registration Indexes. London, England: General Register Office. © Crown copyright.

Soldiers died in the Great War [database on-line].
Ancestry.com, Provo, UT, USA: Ancestry.com Operations Inc, 2008. Original data: British and Irish Military Databases. The Naval and Military Press Ltd.

British Army WWI Service Records, 1914-1920 [database on-line].
Ancestry.com, Provo, UT, USA: Ancestry.com Operations Inc, 2008; Original data: The National Archives of the UK (TNA): Public Record Office (PRO); War Office: Soldiers' Documents, First World War 'Burnt Documents' (Microfilm Copies); (The National Archives Microfilm Publication WO363); Records created or inherited by the War Office, Armed Forces, Judge Advocate General, and related bodies; The National Archives of the UK (TNA), Kew, Surrey, England.

British Army WWI Medal Rolls Index Cards, 1914-1920 [database on-line].
Ancestry.com, Provo, UT, USA: Ancestry.com Operations Inc, 2008. Original data: Army Medal Office. WWI Medal Index Cards. In the care of The Western Front Association website.

Soldiers' Effects Records, 1901-60: [database on-line].
Ancestry.com, Provo, UT, USA: Ancestry.com Operations, Inc., 2014. Original data: National Army Museum; Chelsea, London, England

British Army WWI Pension Records 1914-1920 [database on-line].
Ancestry.com, Provo, UT, USA: Ancestry.com Operations Inc, 2010. Original data: The National Archives of the UK (TNA). War Office: Soldiers' Documents from Pension Claims, First World War (Microfilm Copies); [database on-line]. Ancestry.com, Provo, UT, USA: Ancestry.com Operations, Inc., 2014. Original data: National Army Museum; Chelsea, London, England

British Army WWI Pension Records 1914-1920 [database on-line].
Ancestry.com, Provo, UT, USA: Ancestry.com Operations Inc, 2010. Original data: The National Archives of the UK (TNA). War Office: Soldiers' Documents from Pension Claims, First World War (Microfilm Copies); (The National Archives Microfilm Publication WO364); Records created or inherited by the War Office, Armed Forces, Judge Advocate General, and related bodies; The National Archives of the UK (TNA), Kew, Surrey, England.

England & Wales, National Probate Calendar (Index of Wills and Administrations), 1858-1966 [database on-line].
Ancestry.com, Provo, UT, USA: Ancestry.com Operations Inc, 2010. Original data: Principal Probate Registry. Calendar of the Grants of Probate and Letters of Administration made in the Probate Registries of the High Court of Justice in England. London, England © Crown copyright.

REFERENCES

All web addresses given are valid as at 14th June 2018.

INTRODUCTION

1. *https://en.wikipedia.org/wiki/World_War_I_casualties*

2. *https://en.wikipedia.org/wiki/World_War_II_casualties*

3. The figure of 383,718 comprises 244,817 identified burials and 138,901 memorials for the Second World War: see table at page 44 of the Commonwealth War Graves Commission Annual Report, 2013 - 2014, at *http://archive.cwgc.org/GetMultimedia.ashx?db=Catalog&type=default&fname=18%5cf4fe71-aca4-4c29-9a52-1ea0615fd136.pdf*

4. *https://www.hrp.org.uk/tower-of-london/history-and-stories/tower-of-london-remembers/*

5. The total population for Britain in 1911, from census records for that year, was 45.1 million, comprising 4,390,219 for the population of Ireland (see *http://www.nisra.gov.uk/census/Historic_Population_Trends_%281841-2011%29_NI_and_RoI.pdf*, 4,759,445 for the population of Scotland (see *http://www.1911census.org.uk/scotland.htm*) and 36,003,276 for the population of England and Wales (see *http://www.visionofbritain.org.uk/census/table_page.jsp?tab_id=EW1911POP2_M5*).

6. See table at *http://www.visionofbritain.org.uk/unit/10251503/cube/TOT_POP.*

CHAPTER 1. FIVE MEN OF BURGH
PRIVATE HERBERT GEORGE HUGHES

7. 1901 census: Class: RG13; Piece: 1783; Folio: 58; Page: 15

8. *http://armyservicenumbers.blogspot.com/2011/08/black-watch-royal-highlanders-1st-2nd.html*

9. 1911 census: Class: RG14; Piece: 10582; Schedule Number: 39

10. *https://www.cwgc.org/find-war-dead/casualty/63326/hughes,-herbert-george/*

11. *http://www.longlongtrail.co.uk/army/regiments-and-corps/the-british-infantry-regiments-of-1914-1918/royal-highlanders-black-watch/*

12. A History of The Black Watch Royal Highlanders in the Great War 1914-1918, p.223 at *http://lib.militaryarchive.co.uk/library/infantry-histories/library/A-History-of-The-Black-Watch-Royal-Highlanders-in-the-Great-War-1914-1918-Volume-I/index.asp#/223/zoomed*

13. See 12 above

14. See 10 above

15. Deaths Jun 1926, Volume 4a, Page 976

16. Deaths Sep 1935, Volume 4a, Page 975

17. *http://www.lostancestors.eu/memwar/F/Falkland.htm*

18. *https://www.ipswichwarmemorial.co.uk/frederick-john-hughes/*

PRIVATE ALBERT VICTOR LAST

19. Commonwealth War Graves Commission leaflet, Mons to Marne, at *http://issuu.com/wargravescommission/docs/mons_to_marne_leaflet*

20. Statistics of the military effort of the British Empire during the Great War, 1914-1920 (1922), page 253 (at *https://*

archive.org/details/statisticsofmili00grea),
Great Britain, War Office, London,
H.M. Stationery Office, 1922

21. *http://www.bl.uk/world-war-one/articles/
voluntary-recruiting*

22. *http://www.bbc.co.uk/schools/
worldwarone/hq/hfront1_01.shtml*

23. Sarah Webb: The First World War
with Imperial War Museum at *https://
en.wikipedia.org/wiki/Recruitment_to_
the_British_Army_during_the_First_
World_War*

24. *http://www.1914-1918.net/suffolks.htm
http://www.longlongtrail.co.uk/army/
regiments-and-corps/the-british-infantry-
regiments-of-1914-1918/suffolk-regiment/*

25. See service records of, eg., Private
Herbert William Brooks of the 9th
Battalion, Suffolk Regiment, service
number 15036, enlisted 12 September
1914; and, Private John Frederick
Barber of the 9th Battalion, Suffolk
Regiment, service number 15099,
enlisted 14 September 1914 at
Ancestry.com

26. For details of the work of signallers at
the front, see: *http://www.reasignals.net/
wordpress/army-signals-in-world-war-
one-and-the-role-of-the-royal-engineers/*

27. *http://goodchilds.org/edmund-leonard-
ned/*. The mention of George Chaplin
may perhaps refer to Private Charles
George Chaplin of the 2nd Battalion,
Suffolk Regiment, killed in action 20
December 1914, who was from Kirton;
or to Private H. Henry George Chaplin
of the 4th Battalion, Suffolk Regiment,
killed in action 22 January 1915, who

enlisted at Leiston.

28. See 27 above

29. pp.93-4, History of the Suffolk
Regiment 1914-1927; Lieut -Col
C. C. R. Murphy (1928) London,
Hutchinson and Co. (Publishers) Ltd.

30. *http://www.longlongtrail.co.uk/battles/
battles-of-the-western-front-in-france-
and-flanders/the-battle-of-loos/*

31. See 29 above

32. National Archives ref. WO95-1625-1_1

33. See, eg., *http://en.wikipedia.org/wiki/
Arthur_Frederick_Saunders*

34. See 30 above

35. *http://westfrontassoc.mtcdevserver.
com/the-great-war/great-war-on-land/
battlefields/3132-the-suffolk-regiment-at-
the-battle-of-loos.html#sthash.3Zixim81.
dpbs*

36. pp.123-4, History of the Suffolk
Regiment 1914-1927; Lieut -Col
C. C. R. Murphy (1928) London,
Hutchinson and Co. (Publishers) Ltd.

37. Captain Ensor was subsequently
wounded on the Somme (in the same
action as William Chenery died)
and invalided out of the Army: see
*http://www.ensors.co.uk/documents/
anniversary_book_final_web_version.pdf*

38. See 27. Above

39. See, eg., Stanley Last's medal card,
British Army WWI Medal Rolls Index
Cards, 1914- 1920

40. England & Wales, Death Index, 1916-
2007

41. See 40 above

LANCE CORPORAL WILLIAM

GLADSTONE CHENERY

42. Married 4th Quarter, 1884, Bosmere Registration District, volume 4a, page 1331

43. For Alice, see 1891 census for Kirton. Class RG12; Piece 1476; Folio 36; Page 12; GSU roll: 6096586

44. Alice was in domestic service at Ufford in 1901 and in Ipswich in 1911.
1901 census: Class: RG13; Piece: 1785; Folio: 122; Page: 20
1911 census: Class: RG13; Piece: 1785; Folio: 122; Page: 20

45. 1911 census for Burgh: Class RG14; Piece 10866; Schedule Number 74

46. *http://armyservicenumbers.blogspot.co.uk/2009/07/suffolk-regiment-1st-2nd-battalions.html*

47. *http://www.longlongtrail.co.uk/army/regiments-and-corps/the-british-infantry-regiments-of-1914-1918/suffolk-regiment/*

48. *http://goodchilds.org/the-letters/*

49. page 28, Booth's Almanac for 1916, at Suffolk Record Office

50. pp.125, History of the Suffolk Regiment 1914-1927; Lieut -Col C. C. R. Murphy (1928) London, Hutchinson and Co. (Publishers) Ltd.

51. see *https://en.wikipedia.org/wiki/Battle_of_Verdun*

52. *https://www.cwgc.org/history-and-archives/first-world-war/campaigns/western-front/the-somme*

53. *http://media.cwgc.org/media/244555/the_somme_information_leaflet.pdf*

54. pp.195, History of the Suffolk Regiment 1914-1927; Lieut -Col C. C. R. Murphy (1928) London, Hutchinson and Co. (Publishers) Ltd.

55. See 32 above

56. See 32 above

57. The British Campaign in France and Flanders, Vol. III, Arthur Conan Doyle(1918) Hodder & Stoughton, London, at *http://gutenberg.net.au/ebooks12/1202571h.html#chap10*

58. *http://www.cwgc.org/find-war-dead/casualty/1543394/CHENERY,%20WILLIAM%20GLADSTONE*

59. *http://www.cwgc.org/*

60. *http://www.nationalarchives.gov.uk/pathways/firstworldwar/battles/somme.htm*

61. *http://www.bbc.co.uk/history/worldwars/wwone/nonflash_map.shtml*

62. Death registered March 1926 at Woodbridge Registration District: volume 4a, page 1193

63. Death registered September 1939 at Deben Registration district, volume 4a, page 1358

SERGEANT HORACE WILLIAM SHERMAN

64. 1901 census: Class: RG13; Piece: 1782; Folio: 105; Page: 5

65. 1911 census: Class: RG14; Piece: 10866; Schedule Number: 81

66. FreeBMD Marriage Index, 1837-1915 [database on-line]

67. *http://www.thewardrobe.org.uk/research/history-of-regiments/the-duke-of-edinburghs-wiltshire-regiment-1881-1920-the-wiltshire-regiment-duke-of-edinburghs-1920-1959].*

68. The 2nd Battalion Wiltshire Regiment (99th): A Record of Their Fighting in the Great War, 1914-1918 (1927)

REFERENCES

Major W Scott Shepherd), Gale and Polden, Aldershot

69. See 68 above

70. See 68 above

71. Horace junior's date of birth is confirmed in the registration of his death; England & Wales, Civil Registration Death Index, 1916-2007

72. *http://www.longlongtrail.co.uk/army/regiments-and-corps/the-british-infantry-regiments-of-1914-1918/the-duke-of-edinburghs-wiltshire-regiment/*

73. p.418, The campaign in Mesopotamia, 1914-1918 (vol. II) (1924) Moberly, F. J., London, H.M. Stationery Office

74. *http://www.thewardrobe.org.uk/research/war-diaries/detail/13020*

75. See, eg., the biography of General Townshend at p.289 Who's Who in World War I (2001) Bourne, J.M., London, Routledge

76. *http://www.thewardrobe.org.uk/research/war-diaries/detail/13212*

77. *http://www.nam.ac.uk/online-collection/detail.php?acc=1965-10-221-85*

GUNNER ROBERT BROOM

78. FreeBMD. England & Wales, FreeBMD Birth Index, 1837-1915

79. *http://www.longlongtrail.co.uk/army/regiments-and-corps/the-royal-artillery-in-the-first-world-war/the-siege-batteries-of-the-royal-garrison-artillery/*

80. *http://www.cgsc.edu/CARL/nafziger/918BKWB.pdf*

81. search at *http://www.cwgc.org/*

82. At *http://www.gutenberg.org/files/36213/36213-h/36213-h.htm*

83. search at *http://www.cwgc.org/*

THE END OF THE WAR

84. *http://en.chateauversailles.fr/discover/history/key-dates/treaty-versailles-1919*

TWO FURTHER CASUALTIES

85. search at *http://www.cwgc.org/*

THE DEDICATION OF THE WAR MEMORIAL

86. *https://historicengland.org.uk/whats-new/first-world-war-home-front/what-we-already-know/land/war-memorials/*

87. The East Anglian Daily Times, Monday, 29th September 1919, on microfilm at Suffolk Record Office

BURGH'S WORLD WAR II FALLEN PRIVATE HARRY PATERNOSTER

88. England & Wales, Birth Index, 1916-2005: Date of Registration: Apr-May-Jun 1921; Registration district: Woodbridge; Volume Number: 4a; Page Number: 2008

89. FreeBMD Birth Index, 1837-1915 Registration Year: 1915; Registration Quarter: Jan-Feb-Mar; Registration district: Woodbridge; Volume: 4a; Page: 2008

90. England & Wales, Marriage Index, 1916-2005: Date of Registration: Jul-Aug-Sep 1939; Registration district: Deben; Volume Number: 4a; Page Number: 5359

91. Date of Registration: Jul 1997; Age at Death: 82; Registration district: Ipswich; Register Number: C17B; District and Subdistrict: 7471C; Entry Number: 209

92. Birth Index, 1916-2005: Date of

Registration: Oct-Nov-Dec 1919;
Registration district: Woodbridge;
Volume Number: 4a; Page Number:
2079

93. Date of Registration: Sep 1994; Age
at Death: 75; Birth Date: 15 Sep
1919; Registration district: Ipswich;
Register Number: C11B; District and
Subdistrict: 7471C; Entry Number:
166

94. *https://www.cwgc.org/find-war-dead/
casualty/2114296/paternoster,-harry/*

95. Jiggered about Beyond Belief: Layforce
1941 Alan Orton with Mike Beckett:
at *http://gallery.commandoveterans.org/
cdoGallery/d/32707-17/Layforce.pdf*

96. See 93 above
97. See 93 above
98. See 93 above

SERGEANT DESMOND CLAUDE
YOUNGS

99. Date of Registration: Oct-Nov-Dec
1923 Registration district: Ipswich
Volume Number: 4a
Page Number: 1680

100. Date of Registration: Jul-Aug-Sep 1916
Registration district: Ipswich Volume
Number: 4a Page Number: 1888

101. Date of Registration: Jul-Aug-Sep 1919
Registration district: Ipswich Volume
Number: 4a Page Number: 1577

102. Probate Date: 25 Jan 1945 Death
Date: 24 Mar 1944 Death Place:
Suffolk, England Registry: Ipswich;
Principal Probate Registry. Calendar
of the Grants of Probate and Letters of
Administration made in the Probate
Registries of the High Court of Justice

in England. London, England ©
Crown copyright

103. Date of Registration: Mar 1943 Age at
Death: 56 Registration district: Deben
Inferred County: Suffolk Volume: 4a
Page: 1465

104. *http://www.cwgc.org/find-war-dead/
casualty/2101426/YOUNGS,%20
DESMOND%20CLAUDE*

105. Chapter 11, The Berlin Raids, R.A.F.
Bomber Command Winter 1943-44
(1988) Martin Midlebrook, London,
Viking (Penguin Group)

106. page 59, RAAF fatalities in Second
World War among RAAF personnel
serving on attachment in Royal Air
Force squadrons and support units
(2006) Alan Storr, Canberra, Australia,
Kwik Kopy Canberra

107. *http://www.rafcommands.com/Ross/
Air%20Force%20PoWs/RAF%20
POWs%20Query%20M_1.html*

108. *https://visionpdf.com/raaf-personnel-
serving-on-attachment-in-royal-air-fo
rce77cb53b0d0db3aa2e23613ca24
9a284742934.html*

109. As 103 above

PRIVATE ARTHUR HENRY WOODS

110. FreeBMD Birth Index, 1837-1915:
Registration Quarter: Oct-Nov-Dec
1907; Registration district: Bosmere;
Volume: 4a; Page: 955

111. 1911 census: Class: RG14; Piece:
10763; Schedule Number: 55

112. Date of Registration: Jul-Aug-Sep 1940;
Registration district: Ipswich; Volume
Number: 4a; Page Number: 4541

113. FreeBMD Birth Index, 1837-1915:

Registration Quarter: Apr-May-Jun 1912; Registration district: Woodbridge; Volume: 4a; Page: 1983

114. England & Wales, National Probate Calendar (Index of Wills and Administrations), 1858-1966 Probate Date: 17 Jul 1946; Death Date: 28 Jan 1945; Registry: Ipswich.

115. https://www.cwgc.org/find-war-dead/casualty/2221712/woods,-arthur-henry/

116. http://www.suffolkregimentmuseum.co.uk/brief-history-of-the-regiment/

117. see, eg., http://www.roll-of-honour.org.uk/s/html/savin-kenneth.html

118. https://en.wikipedia.org/wiki/Battle_of_Singapore

119. https://www.cofepow.org.uk/armed-forces-stories-list/the-story-of-changi

120. See 'TO' column of spreadsheet at https://drive.google.com/file/d/0BwYC2zir-F9VWmxUN0NFWVJpVm8/view

121. See page 54 of 87 of the Japanese prisoner of war rosters at http://www.mansell.com/pow_resources/Formosa/TAIWAN_POW_Camp_rosters_RG331Bx1322.pdf. The date in the final column, under 'Remarks', 14/11/17 is 14 November 1942, 1942 being the 17th year of the Japanese 'Showa' era.

122. http://www.west-point.org/family/japanese-pow/ShipsNum.htm (Takao is a port in Taiwan)

123. http://ww2today.com/29th-october-1942-the-hell-of-a-japanese-prison-ship

124. Taichu and Kinkaseki camps are listed in searching for Arthur in the index at http://www.powtaiwan.org/The%20Men/index.php. The list includes a third camp for him – Shirakawa, for which further details are given in the text above.

125. http://www.powtaiwan.org/The%20Camps/camps_detail.php?Taiwan-POW-Camp-2---Taichu-5&name=Taichu

126. http://www.powtaiwan.org/The%20Camps/camps_detail.php?Kinkaseki-POW-Camp-1

127. https://www.cofepow.org.uk/armed-forces-stories-list/kinkaseki-copper-mine-taiwan (Kagi is in Taiwan, not Japan)

128. http://www.powtaiwan.org/The%20Camps/camps_detail.php?Taiwan-POW-Camp-4A---Shirakawa-8&name=Shirakawa

129. http://www.powtaiwan.org/The%20Men/men_honour.php?page=43

130. see page 123 of 142 at http://www.mansell.com/pow_resources/Formosa/TAIWAN_Deaths_RG407Bx190.pdf

131. seen at http://www.antiqbook.com/search.php?action=search&l=en&owner_id=csmx&full=James+William+Hugo, but link no longer working, August 2018

132. http://www.cwgc.org/find-a-cemetery/cemetery/2000320/SAI%20WAN%20WAR%20CEMETERY

133. (Elijah Woods) Date of Registration: Dec 1948; Age at Death: 78; Registration district: Ipswich; Volume: 4b; Page: 717

134. (Minnie Woods (neé Jacobs)) Date of Registration: Sep 1949 Age at Death: 67 Registration district: Ipswich Inferred County: Suffolk Volume: 4b Page: 604

135. Date of Registration: Oct-Nov-Dec

1951 Registration district: Deben
Volume Number: 4b
Page Number: 1486

136. Date of Registration: Nov 1994 Age at
Death: 82 Registration district: Deben
Register Number: 18C District and
Subdistrict: 7431 Entry Number: 57

137. Date of Registration: Jan 2000 Age at
Death: 77 Registration district: Ipswich
Register Number: D25B District and
Subdistrict: 7471D

A FURTHER SECOND WORLD
WAR CASUALTY ASSOCIATED
WITH BURGH

138. search at *http://www.cwgc.org/*

THE SECOND WORLD WAR ROLL
OF HONOUR

139. *https://heritage.suffolk.gov.uk/Data/
Sites/1/media/parish-histories/burgh.pdf
and http://www.visionofbritain.org.uk/
unit/10251503/cube/TOT_POP*

ILLUSTRATIONS

fig. 1 Burgh War Memorial, Burgh Church,
Drabbs Lane, Burgh, Suffolk

fig. 2 Herbert Hughes in 1891 census for
Falkenham, Suffolk. 1891 census:
Class: RG12; Piece: 1475; Folio: 83;
Page: 12; GSU roll: 6096585.

fig. 3 Herbert Hughes in 1901 census for
Woodbridge, Suffolk. 1901 census:
Class: RG13; Piece: 1786;
Folio: 73; Page: 7.

fig. 4 Herbert Hughes in 1911 census for the
2nd Battalion Black Watch, serving in
India. 1911 census: Class: RG14; Piece:
34987; Page: 2.

fig. 5 Soldiers' Effects Record showing

Herbert Hughes' death from wounds at
Casualty Clearing Hospital
Number 6, Bethune
Soldiers' Effects Records, 1901-60;
NAM Accession Number: 1991-02-
333; Record Number Ranges: 185501-
187000; Reference: 76

fig. 6 Bethune Town Cemetery in 1915,
from *http://battlefields1418.50megs.com/
loos_photos.htm*

fig. 7 Bethune Town Cemetery today, from
*http://www.cwgc.org/find-a-cemetery/
cemetery/6000/BETHUNE%20
TOWN%20CEMETERY*

fig. 8 Gravestone record for Herbert Hughes,
from *http://www.cwgc.org/find-war-
dead/casualty/63326/HUGHES,%20
HERBERT%20GEORGE*

fig. 9 1901 Census showing the Last family
in barracks at Cardiff.
1901 census: Class: RG13; Piece: 4982;
Folio: 163; Page: 2

fig. 10 1911 Census showing the Last family
at Burgh
1911 census: Source Citation: Class:
RG14; Piece: 10866; Schedule
Number: 68

fig. 11 Old postcard photograph of the Post
Office, Burgh: courtesy of Burgh
Church

fig. 12 A poster with the famous image of
Lord Kitchener encouraging volunteers
to join up: "Kitchener-leete" by
Alfred Leete. Licensed under Public
Domain via Wikimedia Commons
- *http://commons.wikimedia.org/wiki/
File:Kitchener-leete.jpg#mediaviewer/
File:Kitchener-leete.jpg*. In fact, this
image did not appear in poster form
until the end of September 1914, by

which time voluntary enlistments had already passed their peak. The biggest spur to recruitment appears to have been early reports of British setbacks in France (see The Impact of Mons, August 1914, by John Terraine, published in , Volume 14, Issue 8, August 1964; online at: *http://www. historytoday.com/john-terraine/impact-mons-august-1914)*

fig. 13 Shoreham Camp (at *http://goodchilds. org/edmund-leonard-ned/#enlistment)*

fig. 14 The attack through a cloud of poison gas on the opening day of the Battle of Loos, 25 September 1915 (c) Imperial war Museum, ref. HU_63277B

fig. 15 Extract of war diary of the 9th Battalion, Suffolk Regiment, for their attack at Loos, 25-26 September 1915. National Archives ref. WO 95/1625/1

fig. 16 Extract of war diary of the 9th Battalion, Suffolk Regiment, for 30 December 1915. National Archives ref. WO 95/1625/1

fig. 17 Announcement of the death of Albert Last, Suffolk Chronicle and Mercury, 7th January 1916. Image courtesy of Suffolk Record Office

fig. 18 Captain Lionel Ike Ensor: courtesy of Ensors Chartered Accountants

fig.19 Local newspaper report of Albert Last's death, 1916. *https://www.friendsofthesuffolkregiment.org/ operation-legacy/casualties-or-killed-1* citing the Suffolk branch Western Front Association monthly newsletter

fig. 20 White House Cemetery, St. Jean-les-Ypres, Belgium *http://www.cwgc.org/find-a-cemetery/ cemetery/52400/WHITE%20*

HOUSE%20CEMETERY,%20ST.%20 JEAN-LES-YPRES

fig. 21 The grave of Private Albert Victor Last, White House Cemetery, Ypres: *http:// www.findagrave.com/cgi-bin/fg.cgi?page= gr&GRid=12327778&ref=acom*

fig. 22 Sheet including inscription requested for Albert Last's headstone by his father: *http://www.cwgc.org/find-war-dead/casualty/454721/LAST,%20 ALBERT%20VICTOR*

fig. 23 Family memorial to Albert Last in the Suffolk Chronicle and Mercury of 11 January 1918: courtesy of Suffolk Record Office

fig. 24 The Chenery family at Burgh in the 1901 Census
1901 census: Class: RG13; Piece: 1782; Folio: 105; Page: 5

fig. 25 Private William Chenery of the 2nd Battalion, Suffolk Regiment, at Aldershot Barracks, 1911 Census
1911 census: Class: RG14; Piece: 3122

fig. 26 Felixstowe Garrison football team containing Lance Corporal Chenery in the Bedfordshire Times and Independent, 16 April 1915 at *http://www. britishnewspaperarchive.co.uk/viewer/ bl/0000749/19150416/114/0007.* Image © Johnston Press plc. Image created courtesy of The British Library Board.

fig. 27 Map of the Battle of Flers-Courcelette, Somme Campaign, highlighting The Quadrilateral *https://twcopeman.wordpress. com/2013/11/18/thomas-son-albert/*

fig. 28 British tank at the Battle of Flers-Courcelette, Somme, 15 September

ACKNOWLEDGMENTS

I would like to thank the following, who have provided information about the men, helped me with my researches and in writing up this publication and for their support and encouragement:

The National Archives

Ancestry.com

The British Newspaper Archive online

Great War Forum: *http://1914-1918. invisionzone.com/forums/index.php*

Wiltshire County Council

The Rifles Berkshire and Wiltshire Museum: *www. thewardrobe.org.uk/*

Wiltshire and Swindon History Centre, Cocklebury Road, Chippenham, Wiltshire SN15 3QN

Wiltshire Museum, 41 Long Street, Devizes SN10 1NS: *www. wiltshiremuseum.org.uk/*

The late Roger Mansell, decd. And his colleagues, for the materials from his collection on Allied Prisoners of War of the Japanese, accessible at *http://www. mansell.com/pow-index.html*

COFEPOW, the organisation for the children, families and friends of Far East Prisoners of War and their website at *https://www. cofepow.org.uk/*

The FEPOW Family and Community, accessible with many other links concerning

Far East Prisoners of War via the website *http://www.fepow.family/index.htm*

Burgh Parish Meeting

Adam and Gillian Gurdon

Reverend Wendy Gourlay

Edward Creasy

Sally Butler

Sheila Brechin

Grundisburgh News

Ronald Last and Leslie Last

John Tomalin of Ensors, Chartered Accountants

Dianne Driscoll

Henry Finch *(www.goodchilds.org)*

Paul Reed

Chris Clarke and Jane Newley

District Councillor Tony Fryatt and Suffolk Coastal District Council for their financial assistance and support, by way of a grant from their Enabling Communities Budget

The Wood Trust Burgh for their further financial assistance towards getting this book published

The many other websites and books and their authors and creators that I have consulted, with apoloogies for not being able to list them all

...and last, but not least, my family for bearing with me over the last 4 years and for their active help in putting this book together.

Any corrections and additions can be sent to *EHPubCo@gmail.com*

Published in the United Kingdom by
Edgar's House Publishing

First printing, 2018
Book design by Alice Hines
ISBN 978-1-9993084-0-7

Sponsored by
Suffolk Coastal District Council
and The Wood Trust Burgh